Mandatory Celibacy in the Catholic Church

A Handbook for the Laity

Michele Prince

New Paradigm Books
Pasadena, California

Copyright © 1992 by Michele Prince

New Paradigm Books
P. O. Box 60008
Pasadena, California 91116 - U.S.A.

Cover design - Greg Endries

Printed in the U.S.A. on acid-free paper.

Library of Congress Cataloging-in-Publication Data

Prince, Michele, 1946-
     Mandatory celibacy in the Catholic Church : a handbook for
the laity / Michele Prince.
         p.   cm.
     ISBN 0-932727-60-3 (pbk.) : $9.95 -- ISBN 0-932727-61-1
(library hard cover) : $14.95
     1. Celibacy--Catholic Church. 2. Catholic Church--Clergy.
I. Title.
BV4390.P75 1992
253'.2--dc20   92-16145
                                         CIP

For my daughter Felicity, in the hope that she will inherit a better world.

Acknowledgments

I am deeply grateful to my family for their emotional support and patience when I was irritable or preoccupied.

I want also to thank the many people, mentioned in the text or unmentioned, who helped or encouraged me during the writing of this book and its publication.

Introduction

Without the negative life experiences that I as a woman have had in the Catholic Church during the last 15 years—experiences which I perceive as inseparable from the requirement of compulsory celibacy for Catholic priests—this book would not have been written. But rather than choosing to leave the Church, I chose to write this book in the hope of transforming my experience into a positive force for change.

It has been made clear to me both through these experiences and through input received during the process of composition that change in the rule of celibacy must begin with the laity, who must demand change. Their decision can be ratified later by the hierarchy.

The book was written with growing awareness of other critical realities. The problem of celibacy is the greatest crisis the Catholic Church has faced since the Reformation, and how it is resolved may decide its survival—at least in its present form. The Church worldwide is severely handicapped by the mandating of celibacy for priests, but the life of the American Church is probably the most immanently endangered. As perhaps the most critical part of this danger, the failure to confront the crisis and make needed change is inevitably becoming a threat to the unity of the Catholic Church, both in the United States and worldwide.

Despite its position and some of its content, the basic spirit of the book is meant to be one of compassion for priests, many of whom, at the time of ordination, have only an incomplete, intellectual understanding of what they are really taking on. The lack of sexual expression is often the least of their future problems, but it's all part of one big package, and one that they are often emotionally unprepared to receive. I'm not without compassion for bishops either, though this also may be less than obvious. As a retired bishop told me, perhaps the main source of their reluctance to confront the need for change is a sense that they have painted themselves into a corner on celibacy, and don't know how to get out. Perhaps my insight and those of other laypeople can provide a beginning solution to their dilemma.

But as the first inescapable step out of their "corner," the hierarchy must decide to hear the will of the people. To continue to ignore their voice can only lead to escalating disaster.

Ultimately, this book was written in the hope of helping to motivate the Catholic laity to make themselves heard on this issue—and too loudly to be ignored.

Table of Contents

1

Theological and ◆
Historical Issues Related
to Mandatory Celibacy

*"What I say to you in the darkness, speak in the light:
what you hear whispered, proclaim on the housetops."
(Matthew 10:27)*

Upon investigation it has been made clear to me and to a number of others that the concept of obligatory celibacy for those in priestly ministry did not originate in Christianity. The Roman Catholic Church[1] has given this idea a Christian rationale or covering, but this does not alter the facts of origin.

The Catholic Church's expectation that a priest should observe "ritual purity" (refrain from sexual intercourse) before celebrating Mass goes back to the fourth century A.D., yet this concept cannot be found in Scripture or directly in the Jewish tradition.

---

[1]   Hereafter the generally accepted term, Catholic church, will be used to refer to the Roman church.

There is a text in the Old Testament[2] that states that "if a man lies with a woman, they shall both bathe in water and be unclean until evening." According to Orthodox Rabbi Jonathan Seidemann at Ner Israel Rabbinical College in Baltimore, this text referred to any 24-hour period and also pertained to priests before leading worship. However, he stressed that bathing was a ritual activity expressing spiritual purity, rather like the handwashing gesture of priests at the beginning of Mass. In the Jewish tradition legitimate (marital) sexual activity has never been associated with any idea that it is sinful or unclean. Rabbi Seidemann further claimed that the Jewish tradition views celibacy as "against the intent of creation" and another rabbi at the Talmudical Academy in Baltimore emphasized that there is no celibate tradition in Judaism.

The Levitical text seems to suggest that what may also have been in the mind of Yahweh was the desirability of maintaining at least a basic level of physical cleanliness among the Chosen People by connecting bathing with sexual activity.

Nothing in the Old Testament specifically governs the sexual conduct of priests except for the precept that a priest may not marry a widow or a divorced person unless she was the widow of a priest.[3] Interestingly enough, there is a specific prohibition on alcohol consumption by priests before leading worship;[4] the implied

---

[2] Leviticus 15:18.
[3] Leviticus 21:13-14; Ezekiel 44:22.
[4] Leviticus 10:8-9.

reason in the next verse is that this might impair the priest's ability to conduct worship with due reverence. This prohibition is also found in Ezekiel 44:21.

There is a New Testament text[5] that seems to have a direct application to this issue, as the later historical perspective will clarify. To paraphrase, Paul predicts that in later times some demonically influenced groups will turn away from the Faith and "forbid marriage." In the next verse, Paul repudiates this teaching because "everything created by God is good and nothing is to be rejected when received with thanksgiving, for it is to be made holy by the invocation of God in prayer." This is an unusual text for St. Paul and it appears out of context with the rest of the epistle. It seems likely that, while thinking and writing about other matters (or dictating to someone else), he suddenly received a separate revelation of future events. The first verse of the text itself confirms this interpretation.

Marriage was elevated to an unprecedentedly high level by Jesus and by the early Church. However, the association of women and sexuality with darkness and evil predates Christianity and can be found in various cultures. A number of ancient and pre-Christian societies practiced "cultic purity:" the requirement that sacrifice offerers must remain untainted by sexual encounters.[6] Examples were the Vestal Virgins of ancient Rome who were forced into celibacy and social isolation in a sort of

---

[5] 1 Timothy 4:1-4.

[6] Richard Sipe, *A Secret World: Sexuality and the Search for Celibacy*, Brunner/Mazel, 1990: p. 35.

cloister, frequently by familial expectation, to tend the sacred fire (pray for their society).

The Druids were a religious order in ancient Britain and elsewhere who may have been celibate, though according to Dr. Gavin Langmuir of Stanford University's history department, no reliable information exists on this point. They were certainly set apart by dress and custom. The memory of the Druids' priestly tradition in their collective unconscious could have been one reason the Irish were so receptive to St. Patrick.

Aztec temple priests were also expected to remain sexually abstinent. Like the priesthood itself, the idea that a blood sacrifice must be made to atone for sin might be regarded as an ancient archetype—or part of the intuitive knowledge of the human race. The Old Testament required numerous animal sacrifices, but human sacrifice was strictly forbidden.

Psychologist Carl Jung may not have specifically mentioned the celibate priesthood but it would not be difficult to include this in his concept of "the collective unconscious."[7] The preconscious fantasy of the *vagina dentata* is discovered in many primitive societies and is sometimes found in patients undergoing analysis today. There is an association of this fantasy with fears of castration and injury and—in the psychological sense—fears of psychic injury and domination by women.[8] Or, as Sipe expresses it, "Freud's . . . concept of the universality

---

[7] *Encyclopedia Britannica,* William Benton, 1959: vol. 13, p. 184.

[8] Theodore Lidz, *The Person: His Development throughout the Life Cycle,* Basic Books, 1968: p. 336.

of the 'repudiation of femininity' was based upon castration anxiety . . . it may be, perhaps, more accurately interpreted as the repudiation of the pregenital mother, 'the most ancient enemy.' "[9] The ancient legend of the mermaid who lured sailors to death on the rocks by her beautiful song is another myth expressing in symbolic terms an unconscious fear of women as dangerous and destructive.

Though the theology of Hinduism is not notably misogynistic, Hindu mythology contains elements of this primordial fear. The goddess Kali or "dark mother"—female personification of death and destruction—is usually depicted with four arms, wearing a necklace of skulls. The origins of this devotion are obscure. It could be regarded as a projection of the collective unconscious of the ancient Hindus.[10] Elements of this fear of the female gender are also contained in ancient Taoism with its Yin-Yang duality. Yin (the feminine principle) is identified with the negative cosmic force; Yang (the masculine principle) is identified with the opposing positive force.

To summarize, we can posit that misogyny—fear and rejection of women and femininity and their association with evil and darkness—is a pagan concept. It can be found as a component of both the individual unconscious mind and the collective unconscious. Traces of misogyny can be found in many societies, both ancient and modern.

---

[9]   Ibid., p. 192.
[10]   *Encyclopedia Britannica*, vol. 13, p. 244, Ripley's "Believe It Or Not" Museum, San Antonio, Texas.

This dark corner of the human mind may in fact be universal, as Freud seems to have intuitively sensed.

Another major source of the disturbing undercurrent of misogyny in the Catholic Church is ancient Greek philosophy. An examination of the history of theological development makes clear (and it is difficult to overestimate the importance of this) that from approximately the fourth to the 13th centuries prodigious efforts were made by Catholic theologians—including St. Ambrose, St. Augustine and St. Thomas Aquinas—to reconcile or synthesize Christianity with Greek philosophy.

With the benefit afforded by hindsight, this is seen to be an impossible task. Enmeshed in classical Greek thought are many elements of the rejection of women, sexuality and the physical world. Aristotle taught that women were inferior to men; Plato, Aristotle and Hippocrates regarded the sexual act as dangerous and harmful to health. Seneca taught that sexual pleasure is intrinsically evil and permissible only for reproduction. Greek thinkers were demonstrably influenced by the Gnostic belief system and Plato talked of the body as being a prison for the soul.[11]

In contrast, the view of women expressed in both Old and New Testaments and by Jesus himself is remarkably positive—particularly when contrasted with pagan societies and belief systems. Though ancient societies in general treated women harshly, and the Hebrews were

---

[11] Ranke-Heinemann, *Eunuchs for the Kingdom of Heaven,* Doubleday, 1990: pp. 10-15.

no exception, the Old Testament mentions a number of women of strength and valor. Others, such as Delilah, were portrayed as villainesses, but there is in the Old Testament no pervasive view of women as evil, frightening or even as inferiors. The Hebrew taboo on menstruation is sometimes cited as evidence to the contrary, but the Mosaic Law was unusually even-handed. A man who experienced a nocturnal emission was also considered unclean, though for a shorter period of time, and death was the prescribed penalty for both male and female adulterers.[12]

Some of the heroines of the Old Testament achieved distinction through the families they founded. Sarah, wife of Abraham, is the best-known example but there were others. Ruth, through her decision to leave her own country and subsequent marriage to Boaz, became an ancestor of King David and ultimately of Jesus himself. Others were public figures. Deborah, the only recorded female judge of Israel and also a prophetess, is described in Judges 4 and 5 as responsible for Israel's deliverance from Canaanite oppression. She was a figure of morality and stability in an age in which the Israelites were greatly influenced by their pagan neighbors. Esther's intervention, at the risk of her own life, saved the Jewish people from annihilation by King Xerxes (Ahaseurus) of Persia.

The Bible's theology of marriage is also extremely positive. St. Paul declares that the union of husband and wife symbolizes the union between Christ and the

---

[12]   Leviticus 20:10.

Church,[13] though some have accused his teachings of also containing elements of misogyny—perhaps resulting from a negative personal experience in marriage. (It is almost certain that he was married at one time, though he describes himself as single; he was a former Pharisee and marriage was a social expectation.) Throughout his writings, Paul refers to the sexual component of marriage, but conspicuous by its absence is any mention of its companionate purpose. The Genesis account of the first man and woman makes clear, even if we interpret it symbolically, that an equally important reason for marriage as designed by the Creator was to provide the spouses with mutual companionship and support.[14] Although this component of marriage is never specifically mentioned by St. Paul, he does mention the duty of mutual love and of "avoidance of bitterness."[15]

Many Catholic theologians have attempted to attribute a symbolic meaning to the Song of Solomon in the Old Testament: that marriage is used to symbolize Yahweh's love for God's people or even that this book prefigures the oneness of Christ and the Church. When one reads this short book without theological presuppositions, such an interpretation appears farfetched. There is no reason to require the Song of Solomon to be anything other than what it appears to be—an inspired description of married love. The book also contains much practical advice: including a recommendation that romantic love

---

[13] Ephesians 5:29-32.
[14] Genesis 2:18-25.
[15] Colossians 3:19.

should first begin with friendship[16] and emphasizing the necessity of fidelity in marriage.[17]

The most extraordinary claim of Christianity of course is that God not only created our world but entered into it by becoming one of us. Truths inseparable from the realities of Incarnation and Redemption, but still sometimes obscured by theological debate are these: God is the Creator of marriage, the human family and ourselves as sexual beings (in God's infinite ingenuity, reproduction by growing on trees could have been designed) and salvation will ultimately include the body as well as the soul: "We believe in the resurrection of the body and the life of the world to come," though this will not include sexual expression or marriage in its present form.[18]

The Catholic Church's official justification for mandatory celibacy is that it frees the priest for service with an undivided mind. Matthew 19:12 is quoted: "Some men are incapable of sexual activity from birth; some have been deliberately made so; and some there are who have freely renounced sex for the sake of God's reign. Let him accept this teaching who can." However, the theological emphasis has traditionally been on the last part of the verse ("for the sake of God's reign") rather than the first which makes clear that this must be "freely chosen." The Evangelical Counsels or Counsels of Perfection (poverty, chastity and obedience) have this basis in Scripture, and this of course is the way Jesus lived.

---

[16]   2:7.

[17]   4:12.

[18]   Matthew 22:30.

A number of Christian churches have been able to maintain a monastic tradition while allowing, and sometimes preferring, a married clergy. The use of this verse to require that all priests be celibate is a distortion of its original intent. This view is confirmed by the documents of Vatican II which declare that celibacy is not theologically mandated or essential to priesthood but that it is in fact a discipline.[19]

Other texts in Scripture stress the importance of *motive* in God's view of things; "Man looks on the outward appearance but God sees the heart."[20] The incident of the rich man[21] is a familiar example in which Jesus makes clear that renunciation of riches for the sake of the Kingdom of God is associated with perfection. The context also makes clear ("there is one thing left *for you*" and "how hard it is for those who have wealth to enter the Kingdom of God") that the Lord was speaking to this particular person who was apparently too attached to his money, which in turn had become a spiritual stumbling block for him.

Indeed, without considering the motive factor, some saints would have been referred for psychiatric evaluation rather than canonization. A notable example is St. Rose of Lima who died in her early 30s, probably because of a tendency to beat and starve herself. These behaviors appear bizarre without considering the motivation—that

---

[19]   Frank Bonnike, co-founder of CORPUS (Corps of Reserve Priests Organized for Service).
[20]   1 Samuel 16:7.
[21]   Luke 18:18-25.

she was trying to imitate Christ and probably in some way atone for the sins of her society. (It is doubtful that she had many personal sins to report.) In 16th century Peru such actions were considered praiseworthy, if a bit unusual. There was certainly nothing mediocre about St. Rose; according to her lights she gave it the best she had.

Passages from three of the four Gospels[22] reflect Jesus' clear teaching on marriage: it is a sacrament and rightly entered into is indissoluble ("now they are no longer two but one flesh. What God has joined, no man must separate"). An unavoidable conclusion follows from this: while the Evangelical Counsels rightly assumed (by a person who has reached a certain level of psychological maturity and for the Kingdom of God) is a higher calling, a person who is "married in the Lord"[23] might be regarded as holier than one who assumes religious life for the wrong motives. (Motives of course are sometimes unconscious, at least partially).

An additional logical progression results from these texts that can be confirmed by the experience of many priests, both those who remain in ministry and those who leave. When a priest agrees to celibacy because it is a requirement for those who would *attain the end of priesthood* and not because of a personal calling to celibacy or the Evangelical Counsels, this is not a fully free choice. A clarifying analogy is provided by the modern theology of marriage: When a marriage is entered into (marriage

---

[22] Matthew 19:3-9, Mark 10:5-12 and Luke 16:18.
[23] 1 Corinthians 7:39.

vows taken) in which the main goal is not the marriage itself but something else (the spouse's wealth, for example) this is considered by marriage tribunals to be defective consent or grounds for annulment. Such a serious commitment as the vow or promise of celibacy is comparable to the marriage vow and should be taken as an end in itself, not as a means to another end or as part of a job description (for want of a more exact term).

Eugene Kennedy and Victor Heckler's classic study of the American priesthood which was published in 1971 found that a majority of the 271 respondents felt that their choices for celibacy had not been "made in complete freedom."[24] The reported experience of many priests since that study corroborates the dilemma posed by obligatory celibacy—many priests report feeling called to the priesthood but not to single life. A survey taken among American priests records that at least 60 percent favor optional celibacy.[25]

Sipe's research suggests that the conflict sometimes arises after years in ministry: "The priest will want to know eventually if his sexual struggle is with the development of his genuine charism (of celibacy) or if it is a conflict arising from a discipline he accepted as part of his ministerial role without benefit of the special gift."[26]

[24] Fr. Eugene Kennedy, Ph.D. and Victor Heckler, Ph.D., *The Loyola Psychological Study of the Ministry and Life of the American Priest*, p. 16.
[25] CORPUS, *Research Document I*, p. 18.
[26] Sipe, p. 6.

Of course, if Jesus said all priests were to be celibate, that would decide the matter, but the foregoing analysis would demonstrate otherwise. It is doubtful that a petty God or a "respecter of persons" would have chosen to become incarnate.

An examination of the historical development of the celibacy rule in the Catholic Church further clarifies its origin as human—and even influenced by the heresies of the times. In the early days of the Church both married and single persons were welcomed in the clergy and the place of worship was in the home. The early Apostles were married, though Paul is thought to have been a widower, and were often helped by their families in their work of spreading the Gospel. When they "left all to follow Christ," they often took their families with them. Tradition has it that both Peter and his daughter Petronella were martyred and buried in Rome. Many Popes were the sons of Popes; Anastasius I (399-401) was the father of Innocent I; Hormisdas (514-523) was the father of Silverius; and as late as the tenth century, Sergius III (904-911) became the father of John XI.[27]

The early years of Christianity also saw the growth of certain heresies—most notably Gnosticism and Manichaeism. Of pagan origin, both were eventually repudiated by the Christian Church, but not before they were able to exert demonstrable influence on Christian thought. The main heretical elements in Gnosticism resided in the claim that Christ's human nature was not real. Gnostics

---

[27] Sipe, pp. 36-38.

also taught, in common with many pagan philosophies, that "matter" was bad and that there existed an antagonism between soul and body.[28] The two belief systems of Christianity and Gnosticism developed side-by-side and there were reciprocal influences. St. Irenaeus sought to reconcile the two in his writings, but it should be remembered that the Gnostic belief system was in existence before Christianity[29] and was finally condemned by the Council of Nicaea in 325.[30]

Manichaeism has similar beliefs which were introduced in Persia by Mani about 242 A.D. In turn Manichaeism later gave rise to the heresies of Albigensianism or Catharism.[31] During the next hundred years there also existed mutual influences between Manichaeism and Christianity as during the fourth century Manichaeism spread rapidly throughout the Roman Empire. St. Augustine was exposed to its teachings in his early years, though he later rejected them in his writings.

Manichaeism was most successful in gaining support among the clergy in North Africa. Like Gnosticism, it emphasized a strict dualism between matter and spirit. Satan and the Kingdom of Darkness were believed to be real. Adam (the first man) was held to be actually created by Satan. Only a small step is needed from these philosophies to the deduction that sexual activity (the flesh) becomes evil in itself and also because it leads to procre-

---

[28] *Catholic Encyclopedia*, Thomas Nelson Publishers, 1987: p. 242.
[29] *Encyclopedia Britannica*, vol. 10, pp. 453-454.
[30] *Catholic Encyclopedia*, p. 242.
[31] Ibid., p. 369.

ation! The Roman emperors enacted strict laws against the Manichaeans as they were regarded as destructive to the social order. This belief system then went underground, only to reemerge in later centuries in the revived form of Albigensianism.[32]

The decisions of the Church councils have not been made in a social vacuum; neither have the prayer channels to the Holy Spirit remained uncontaminated by popular philosophies and political realities. In the context of the concurrent pagan religious structures and thought, their influence on the Christian Church and the recurrence of certain themes of misogyny in the human unconscious, the mandating of clerical celibacy becomes more comprehensible. The specifics of Canon 33 of the Council of Elvira in 306 also have a diminished shock value:

> Bishops, presbyters, and deacons and all other clerics having a position in the ministry are ordered to abstain completely from their wives and not to have children. Whoever, in fact, does this, shall be expelled from the dignity of the clerical state.

As a matter of practicality, this edict was often modified to the rule that clergy were to abstain from sexual activity before offering Mass. As priests continued to have children, it was clear that the rule was not being observed; this led to the mandating of clerical celibacy in the twelfth century.

---

[32] *Encyclopedia Britannica,* vol. 14, pp. 803-808.

It is surely not coincidental that in the twelfth century there was a revival of Manichaean teaching under the label of Albigensianism. The Albigensians were a politically powerful, organized group that became a force to be reckoned with in France, Italy and Spain. Their tenets included anarchy, anticlericalism—with a call for clergy reform—and abolition of the sacrament of marriage.[33] The French called their leaders *bons hommes* and their anticlerical preaching appealed to the masses.

The fact that a war was fought in France against this group, ending with the Treaty of Paris in 1229, testifies to the strength of the movement and the extent to which, like the Manichaeans, they were regarded as destructive to the social order. Members of the Church hierarchy may have been influenced by the Albigensians or even have been afraid of them. It seems highly improbable that the specific decisions of the Third Lateran Council in 1179 could have been made without reference to this heresy. While officially condemning the Albigensians, the council also called for clergy reform and mandated clerical celibacy.[34]

All marriages by those in Holy Orders were ruled invalid and a wall of separation was erected between the two sacraments. While an official repudiation of the Albigensians was seen as necessary, this law separating marriage and ordination could be viewed as an attempt to appease this popular group. The proceedings of

---

[33]   Ibid., vol. 1, p. 528.
[34]   *Catholic Encyclopedia,* p. 341.

Vatican II with its efforts to conciliate various groups sound a similar note. It seems more than a little strange that the warning of St. Paul in 1 Timothy against permitting any organized group that "forbade marriage" to influence the Church should have been ignored. In enforcing this new rule during the last years of the twelfth century, the Catholic Church did not merely stop ordaining married men, it actually forcibly separated priests and their wives and devised various punishments for the recalcitrant, including the dismissal from the clerical state and the selling of some wives and children of priests into slavery.[35] Predictably, the 14th and 15th centuries saw an increase in scandal and concubinage among the clergy, but sadly, while the male halves of these liaisons were often promoted in the Church hierarchy, the women were frequently persecuted and even denied burial in consecrated ground.[36]

Rather than being a positive good—when seen in this historical context—the mandating of clerical celibacy appears to be a compromise with evil, politically motivated at least in part. The popular admonition is that anyone "who sups with the devil needs a long spoon." When compromise occurs in so intimate a matter, the bill can be due in full centuries later. Ever since the twelfth century the Church has paid a price for mandatory celibacy, but the cost is now unaffordably high and includes the current shortage of vocations, the growing

---

[35] CORPUS, *Research Document I,* 1988, p. 22.
[36] Sipe, pp. 44-45.

numbers of priestless parishes, the many priests depart-
ing from the ministry after ordination and the many si-
lent disillusioned. That the Church has survived celibacy
at all argues more for divine intervention ("I will be with
you all days") than for divine approval of the practice.

However, it is only fair to admit that the celibate
tradition has undoubtedly contributed to the large
religious orders and their concern with social problems as
well as the Church's missionary effort. This can again be
attributed to Divine Ingenuity, "Who is ever able to turn
evil into good."[37] It is unlikely that the monastic tradition of the Evangelical Counsels—which is validated by
Christ himself for certain individuals—would have
attracted so many followers without the emphasis placed
on celibacy by mandating it for priests. However, the
Church is now worldwide and a major focus must be on
consolidating its gains and evangelizing new genera-
tions—efforts which are definitely handicapped by "forbidding marriage" to all priests.

Question for discussion or consideration:

From your experience, what remnants exist in today's Church of the attitude that women and sexual
activity, even within marriage, are unclean or dangerous?

---

[37] St. Thomas More, who was married and the adoptive father of two
daughters, paraphrasing St. Paul.

2

Social Issues Related ♦ to Mandatory Celibacy

"I will strike the shepherd, and the sheep of the flock will be dispersed" (Matthew 26:31).

The most visible effect of the Church's continuing policy is the shortage of priests and seminarians; 42 percent of priests in the United States resign within 25 years after ordination[38] and the number of seminarians has been steadily shrinking: from 40,000 in 1965 to 6,200 today.[39] Though other factors contribute to the diminished number of vocations (the reluctance of many in our society to make commitments, for example) the rule of celibacy is viewed by most sources as the principal reason for the decrease. Throughout the Church it appears that the priesthood is perceived as a valuable vocation and a means of serving the Church and people; but the requirement that to assume the priesthood one has to preclude any personal family life and allow your

---

[38] CORPUS Research Document I, p. 18.

[39] *Time,* September 24, 1990.

profession to become your entire life is seen as unnecessary and unjust.

This view of the rule of celibacy combined with doubts regarding its historical origins is a major factor in the decision of many priests to leave active ministry. They are "voting with their feet," observed a number of resigned priests, including Jack Biondo of Baltimore County—who is married and expecting his first child—and John O'Brien, an officer in the Baltimore chapter of CORPUS who resigned to marry 15 years ago.

Among the resigned there is a pervasive attitude that the Pope and the hierarchy are refusing to admit the need for change, or to deal with the issue at all. The acceptance for ordination of a number of former Episcopalians who were already married is also seen as unjust and discriminatory.[40]

The clergy shortage in the Catholic Church is rapidly reaching the point of crisis in the United States; one church in ten is now without a priest, including at least one in Baltimore. The number of priestless parishes is highest in the western states, but the majority of parishes in other areas have noticed a reduction in the number of clergy assigned to them. A church near Baltimore which had three priests a few years ago, now has only one. The World Synod of Bishops, which met in the Vatican in October of 1990, admitted that there is in fact

---

[40]   Jack Biondo.

a worldwide shortage of priests with some areas being affected more than others.[41]

Representatives to the Second International Congress on a Married Priesthood held in Arricia, Italy in 1987 made a strong statement in favor of the acceptance of married men into the priesthood. The latest statistics on the vocation crisis were also discussed at this congress including the fact that 42 percent of Catholic parishes worldwide were without a full-time priest.[42]

Among the least visible, but still very real, effects of the celibacy crisis is a negative impact on the morale of many priests, and by contagion on their congregations as well. The stress of chronic loneliness plus the possibility of being overwhelmed by other people's problems can cause the priest to be perpetually glum, even in a state of low-grade depression. Since the Catholic laity have been conditioned toward passivity and toward following the lead of those in spiritual authority, a gloomy priest affects them too.

How many joyful, singing congregations are found on a Sunday morning? But just as fish do not notice the water they swim in, this somber atmosphere is frequently taken for granted or goes unnoticed by the congregation. In my personal experience as a cantor or song leader for over a decade in three different parishes, I have experienced limited success in getting the congregation to sing. It was especially difficult to get priests to help animate

---

[41] *The Catholic Review,* October 17, 1990.
[42] From notes taken at the congress by Terry Dosh, co-founder of CORPUS.

the music service. It finally seemed to me, as I decided to give up this effort, that this lack of priestly support might be due to the principle that "misery loves company" and that it is hard to make a joyful noise unto the Lord when you are depressed. The Old Testament contains admonitions against "singing songs to a sorrowful heart," but even some of the bishops' own documents in recent years have noted a morale problem among priests.[43]

Another subtle, but real, effect of forced singleness is that the congregation unwittingly becomes the priest's substitute family. An unfortunate and surely unintended consequence of this is an attitude of: "I'd better be careful not to offend these people." The prophetic role of the priesthood is thus limited, as was portrayed in the movie, "Mass Appeal," which starred Jack Lemmon. Although this was no polemical appeal for optional celibacy, it did point out this problem.

When the prophetic role is avoided, priests fail to deal with the topics that are the basic concerns of the congregation. Homilies on topics such as what the Bible and Church tradition teach about the avoidance of non-marital sex and how to maintain a good marriage and family life are becoming rare in some areas. Valuable opportunities to reverse the breakdown in morality and family life in our country are thus neglected. In contrast, Protestant leaders such as Charles Stanley, former

---

[43] The Bishops' Committee on Priestly Life and Ministry, "The Priest and Stress", p. 8.

president of the Southern Baptist Convention, repeatedly preach sermons on family issues, getting quite specific in their advice. I cannot recall a complete sermon on any of these issues in the Baltimore Catholic Church (which I think is fairly representative of the nation as a whole) in the last ten years, though they are mentioned in passing or as part of an occasional homily.

The Catholic Church now has the highest percentage of single people of any Christian denomination—which is a reversal of recent years. My extensive personal experience in the Catholic singles scene has led me to conclude that many have chosen that life for selfish reasons or due to personal hang-ups, not because they think they can better serve the Lord in that state. Yet rarely are sermons on commitment difficulties ever heard from the Catholic pulpit.

The Archdiocese of Washington, DC—which has the highest percentage of singles in any U.S. city—a few years ago issued a blanket commendation of singleness without any analysis of motives. These are not comfortable topics for Catholic priests and their lack of family support increases their vulnerability. In contrast, such notable Evangelical leaders as Billy Graham are quick to commend their families for their indispensable emotional support. Billy Graham's wife and four adult children certainly have not interfered with his worldwide evangelization campaigns and his son has followed him into the ministry. And Randall Terry, a prolife activist who has now received national attention, states frankly that if it weren't for the fact that he fears for his children's future in a society that is increasingly secular, even rejecting of God, he would have quit long ago. As a fellow activist who has twice been arrested with Operation Rescue, I can see definite parallels between the issues of mandatory celibacy and abortion. Both are topics that are difficult to confront (I can remember an embarrassed tone to some collegiate discussions about abortion) yet the costs to society are enormous. A parallel to the disappearing clergy caused by celibacy is the declining birthrate caused by abortion; early in 1990, the media reported an unexplained decrease in the numbers entering the work force. Though it has now been more than 18 years since the decision, no connection seems to have been made between this fact and Roe vs. Wade.

The difficulty in taking controversial moral positions and in risking the wrath of the media extends to members of the hierarchy as well; they are not immune to the isolation and vulnerability that can be caused by their single state. The support they offer to movements and to groups such as those opposing pornography is sketchy and inconsistent. Valuable opportunities to form coalitions with other Christian groups have been neglected. In the fall of 1990 I attended an antipornography rally sponsored by the American Family Association, a group begun by Evangelicals. Although this rally had been endorsed by the local archbishop, no clergy were in attendance. Perhaps these single people felt out of their element in a group composed mainly of married couples with children.

Another vital issue for the Western Church, which cannot be dealt with apart from a consideration of celibacy and its effects, is that of the role of women. The "gender" question and how the Holy Spirit will lead the

Catholic Church to resolve it was one subject of the Prayer of the Faithful on Sunday, October 21, 1990. The Church can ill afford to ignore this issue indefinitely and still hope to be taken seriously in Western societies where women have been making steady, if albeit slow and uneven, progress.

At the immediate, personal level in many Catholic parishes, women tend to feel excluded, ignored, treated as threats or—though they can't always pinpoint just what—that there is something unhealthy in the attitude of many priests toward them. This is the experience of both single women and married women of my acquaintance. It is not surprising that Sipe's research has revealed that in some cases, the priest appears to have "an unresolved fear of women" which leads him to adopt "a harsh and denigrating attitude toward them that has multiple pastoral and even theological ramifications."[44]

Often women in the Catholic Church report feeling totally discounted in the parish when it comes to decision-making processes. Although they are allowed to volunteer endless hours for caring and sustaining the Church's various functions, should women try to give advice or suggestions—even about the programs they are helping with—they are sometimes met with hostility or even scorn. I recall a particularly unpleasant personal experience: after approximately ten years of unpaid work as a song leader in a certain Baltimore parish, I asked the organist, who had been recently hired, if I could be

---

[44] Sipe, p. 193.

permitted some input into the selection of music for the congregation. I considered the organist, a single man, to be a friend; part of my motivation was a wish to help him as at that time he was a recent convert and had very limited experience with Catholic liturgy. The request was made casually after Sunday Mass; the totally unexpected response was one of hostility and defensiveness and the specific prediction that I "was going to get my feelings hurt." The pastor then interrupted by asking: "Why are you talking to her?" It is as though women are to be seen but not heard, which is reminiscent of Biblical times when Christ's disciples "were surprised he was talking with a woman."[45]

The question remains whether the Church has really changed much since then. Certainly the sexist content of this exchange would be familiar to many Catholic women who have involved themselves in ministry. I left this parish shortly after this incident; to be rejected in effect by a Church I had tried to serve for many years was an experience of great personal pain.

Many anecdotes could be recounted that are illustrative of the discomfort many Catholic priests demonstrate when they are around women. Not only are they often unable to accept even the most innocuous show of friendliness, but often they display a generalized siege mentality. Women report sensing from Catholic priests a certain discomfort bordering on rejection whenever they try to engage in the slightest form of cordial conversation,

---

[45] John 4:27.

as the following incident illustrates. I had moved to another parish and after Mass went to greet a new priest and compliment him on an interesting and enthusiastic sermon. This particular priest was from a southern state and I thought might have some Protestant relatives or have picked up some preaching pointers from the Baptists. He seemed uncomfortable with my greeting and when I asked if he had a Protestant background, he replied, "Certainly not." The tone of his voice and defensive physical posture (he stepped back) reflected hostility and a degree of personal rejection, even though I was a total stranger. In retrospect, I am certain that my gender played a part in this reaction.

Under the Church's current rules, even psychologically healthy priests are forced to distance themselves from women. Treating them in a relaxed, normal manner is difficult because this raises fears of emotional involvement. By viewing women as overly emotional, less intelligent and capable of making decisions, etc., Catholic priests are helped in their personal need for distancing from the "enemy." Thus it is not surprising that a common complaint among women in the Catholic Church is that priests tend to be uninformable, if not downright rude, when women attempt to give input for planning events in the Church or even should they ask for requests that might be outside their ingrained routine. Another incident of about a dozen years ago comes to mind: as an officer of a Catholic singles' club, the Catholic Alumni Club of Baltimore, I asked a Jesuit priest if he would give a retreat for the group and met with him to help organize the event. He made the abrupt suggestion that "if you don't like my ideas, get someone else." As I thought a discussion rather than an argument was taking place, I was taken aback by this response and hastily agreed with the priest's plans. A similar incident occurred when at the request of the same group, I requested another priest to offer a home Mass. I had never previously spoken with the priest and his response, in the presence of others, was one of unprovoked hostility: "I don't have time for this, it's a bad idea, and I can't suggest anyone else either." The request could have been declined with courtesy, and in retrospect I again conclude that my gender was a factor.

The issue of the legitimate role of women is one the Catholic Church can no longer afford to avoid. If change is not forthcoming, certainly it is the Church which will suffer incalculable injury. The situation cannot be corrected within the present structures which unavoidably promote sexism and defensiveness.

Of equal importance is the fact that by forbidding to the Church community the benefits that could be afforded them by the person who is fulfilling the role of the pastor's spouse, the Church is denied a great treasure. As the Catholic population continues to grow and congregations become large and impersonal, with a subsequent loss of any sense of community, many members begin to feel like "numbers" to be counted in the crowd. This point was made by a resigned priest member of CORPUS on the floor of the group's annual convention held in San Jose, California in June of 1990.

If the priest shortage were solved by the ordination of marrieds, there might not be a need for more persons in sacramental ministry, but the contributions of the spouses of priests would still be greatly needed. These potential contributions range from hospitality, home visiting and providing individual attention to parishioners to involvement in specific ministries traditionally filled by ministers' spouses such as music and counseling. Married clergy in many Christian churches admit that even though their spouses are not consistently involved in specific ministries, their very presence adds an aura of hospitality and settledness that is often lacking in the Catholic clergy's situation.

Larry Gesy, a Baltimore priest who conducts seminars on the subject of cults, bemoans the fact that young people are leaving the Catholic Church to join such groups in alarming numbers. He even estimates the membership of some cults to be 70 percent Catholic. In his analysis Fr. Gesy makes a correlation between the lack of demonstrative love and community spirit in so many Catholic churches with the attraction of the young to cultic groups—which all tend to be warm, enveloping, tight-knit and outwardly loving groups—many of which elements seem to be missing in our tradition. It seems clear that the celibacy rule for priests, and its unfortunate consequences, contributes significantly to these deficits.

Another immensely important consideration for the 21st century is that mandatory celibacy is an indirect cause of the defection of minorities, especially Hispanics and Blacks, from the Catholic Church. Again there is a relationship between compulsory celibacy and the lack of community these individuals sometimes feel in Catholic churches. In Latin America in the past two decades the Pentecostal and Evangelical denominations have made tremendous inroads into the ranks of the traditionally Catholic. Now this is happening among Hispanics in the United States as well.

Even those like Mario Paredes, the executive director of the Northeast Hispanic Catholic Center, who personally favors the celibate tradition, support the view that there is an indirect connection between celibacy and Hispanic defection to other Churches. The Pentecostals and Evangelicals offer spontaneous worship, smaller congregations and a "family atmosphere"—an environment many Hispanics find attractive.

Developing a sense of community within the celibate tradition seems to be an impossible task. The shortage of priests results in congregations that are growing ever larger and more impersonal. Though there is nothing intrinsically somber about the Mass, celibacy does contribute to a morale problem, making it difficult for many priests to be joyful or enthusiastic. The denial of marriage and a supportive family setting to priests means that their potential roles as positive models of a Christ-centered family are also denied to the congregation.

As Mr. Paredes also confirmed, the condition of celibacy is an ambiguous one in the Latin culture and its effects may be paradoxical or mixed. Even though in Latin America there are actually many cultures, in general those who are unmarried are seen as suspect individuals and not normative to the society. Traditionally Hispanics have made an exception for the celibate priest, who is often affectionately called *"Padrecito"* (Little Father). At the same time the community has often looked the other way and empathized with those priests who have formed virtually permanent liaisons with acquiescent women.

Simultaneously, many Hispanics continue to regard the priesthood as having a direct line to God and the transcendent. But could this be a form of "kicking the priest upstairs"? It is almost as though by relegating the priest to the realm of the transcendent, it becomes possible to ignore his advice on practical matters such as social justice and the importance of entering and maintaining a sacramental marriage and positive family life. Historically, throughout Latin America, few priests have had much impact on society. This is becoming the trend in our Anglo society as well.

Of course the grievous conditions in Latin America have engendered exceptions to this rule, such as the murdered Archbishop Romero. The state of family life in much of Latin America is alarming. The poorer classes in many Latin countries frequently don't marry in the Church, either because they cannot afford to or because they have no desire to pledge themselves to a permanent commitment. Male desertion of their families is thus often commonplace. In such a macho society it is difficult for men to identify with a celibate priesthood. Hence this contributes, in a subtle way, to decreased Church attendance by males and to the perception that religion—or at least church attendance—is mainly for women. Even though the priest may be revered as a mediator with

God, his celibacy sets him apart and handicaps any effort to achieve credibility as a leader in his society.

Recently the Worldwide Synod of Bishops has reported a slight growth in the number of vocations in Latin American countries. Even so, this growth rate does not begin to keep pace with population growth. To compensate for a frequently absent priesthood, alternate parish programs, such as the Basic Christian Communities, have become increasingly popular in the last few decades. These small groups, usually averaging 15 to 40 members, tend to be led by a three-person team composed of a man, a woman and a young adult. Although these communities retain a direct connection with a priest, the priest does not remain the focal point of the community.[46]

The revolutionary implications of such new structures are enormous. They well could serve either as the transition mode to a married priesthood, or as a step toward the development of a Catholic experience that even further distances the priest from the people. As has happened in some Protestant traditions, the near irrelevance of the ordained clergy and of the sacramental ministry is a not impossible outcome given sufficient time. It is interesting to note that in Mr. Paredes' view, a married clergy would be accepted in most Latin American countries, though as with the changes wrought by Vatican II, there might be some initial resistance.

Also discussed at the Worldwide Synod of Bishops was Pope John Paul II's decision to ordain two married

---

[46] *Catholic Review,* October 24, 1990.

Brazilian men after they agreed to stop living with their wives.[47] How their wives felt about the decision was not reported. This incident alone should remove all doubt concerning the reality of the continued pagan influence on the Church in matters of sexuality. Just as in the twelfth century, the plain words of Christ that "what God has joined, no person must divide" were disregarded.

But should we be surprised or disillusioned to find that an institution as old as the Catholic Church has incorporated elements from the far distant past and acquired a certain amount of excess baggage along the way? God, through the action of the promised Holy Spirit, still remains faithful, continually bringing to light what has been hidden, bending what is rigid and bringing about renewal.

In 1982 Bishop Justin Darwajuomo of Indonesia asked Pope John Paul II in a personal meeting with the pontiff for permission to ordain married men to the priesthood in his country. At that time this bishop offered to resign if such permission was not granted. His resignation was accepted. Beginning in the 1970s, several coalitions of Indonesian bishops had made the same request of the Vatican.[48] All lay catechists in Indonesia are required to be married.

Indonesia is still predominately a Moslem country, with an estimated 85 percent adhering to that religion— a considerable increase from the 60 percent estimate of

---

[47] Ibid.
[48] CORPUS Reports, September-October 1990.

the 1950s. There are some six percent Christians in the population, and an estimated two percent Hindus, with the remainder being Buddhists or animists who believe in many kinds of good and evil spirits. Despite the predominance of Islam, women enjoy a relatively high status in Indonesia and are granted many legal and property rights.[49] There is of course no celibate tradition in Islam and the unmarried state does not enjoy a significant degree of social acceptance in Moslem cultures. A principal cause of these requests by the Indonesian bishops was the perception that clerical celibacy poses not only an obstacle to the Church's missionary effort, but also to the development of native vocations.

The Indonesian experience offers some important lessons to other mission areas of the Church—even those, such as India and Africa, where the celibate tradition might initially have been an asset. Certainly, celibacy serves as a counter-cultural novelty or a sort of attention-getting device. It also allows for more flexibility in the deployment of missionaries. But with the passage of time, the celibacy requirement almost inevitably begins to interfere with the recruitment of adequate numbers of indigenous clergy, evidenced by the worldwide shortage of priests.

All viable societies must value and promote some sort of family structure if they are to remain viable. Significant numbers of individuals might be persuaded to forego this part of life for good and sufficient reason or as a

---

[49] *Encyclopedia Americana*, vol. 15, pp. 79-80.

consequence of a profound faith experience, but this does not occur when forced celibacy begins to be viewed as a nonessential institutional requirement.

The long-term experience with clerical celibacy in the United States is similar, though it may be further advanced than in some other countries. In all societies, visible examples of divergence between theory and practice in the conduct of clergy inevitably lead to some degree of scandal, depending on cultural expectations and tolerance. Ironically, the question of clerical celibacy is largely academic in many African countries where there is a tradition of polygamy. The practical question then becomes how the Catholic Church can limit their priests to one wife![50]

Perhaps similar cultural pressures are coming to bear on the Catholic Church in the United States. After making notable gains among Blacks in recent years, it now finds itself in the position of losing Black membership. This defection is related to celibacy—which is not held in high regard in the Black community. Blacks are accustomed to a married clergy from their Protestant heritage and the minister has traditionally functioned as a cultural leader and as a positive family role model.

The forced resignation in the summer of 1990 of Atlanta's Archbishop Eugene Marino—the first Black to be elevated to this position in America—because of a liaison with Vicky Long did not endear the Church to Black Americans as it removed a representative from the

---

[50]   CORPUS Reports, 1990.

Church hierarchy in whom they felt great pride. The stress of leading a double life coupled with being removed from his profession has apparently brought the former archbishop to the verge of becoming a psychiatric casualty as well. This brouhaha could have been avoided had the archbishop been free to marry Ms. Long who not only attended social functions with him but could have been a solace to him in his pressured position.[51]

If the current demographic trends continue, Blacks and Hispanics will outnumber whites in the United States by the year 2020. The Catholic Church's persistence in policies that are unpopular with or don't meet the needs of these ethnic groups means that its population base for the next century is being eroded.

Related realities of even more critical and immediate impact are the sexual aberrations that are becoming visible in the priesthood: specifically pedophilia and homosexuality. Even though pedophilia is not limited to the Catholic priesthood, still the numerous accusations of such incidents would appear to be directly related to the Church's denial of marriage to priests. This gross misuse of their priestly positions of trust within the community has repeatedly caused girls as young as 13, who may be quite physically mature, to accuse Catholic priests of sexual exploitation. Pedophilia is a rising problem and every year Catholic priests around the country are accused or convicted of statutory rape.

---

[51] *Time,* September 24, 1990.

Certainly the Catholic Church is compounding its own difficulties by allowing this humanly-devised rule to be elevated to its current level so that it is intricately enmeshed—in the eyes of the faithful—with the identity of the Church itself. Elevating a human rule to such a level has the inevitable consequence of attracting to the priesthood a disproportionate number of people with problems.

Dr. Jay R. Feierman, a psychiatrist who has treated 500 sexually abusive priests over a 15-year period, also believes that a rule such as celibacy inevitably attracts too large a percentage of people with a deviant sexual orientation or with the potential for deviance.[52] Richard Sipe's 25-year research in which he interviewed hundreds of priests leads him to conclude that at least 26 percent are either homosexual or attracted to children—this in a society where there is an estimated ten percent of the general population that is homosexual.

Sipe's work, which also deals with a number of priests involved in heterosexual relationships, initially raised a storm of criticism, mainly by the American bishops, but it has since been virtually ignored by the hierarchy. The main focus of the bishops' criticism centered on the fact that, though a large number of priests were interviewed, they represented case histories rather than a random sample. As a professional social worker, I would counter this criticism by noting that it misses the point. Personal and professional experience strongly suggests that people

[52] *Time,* August 19, 1991, p. 51.

are not always honest when dealing with these topics—even with themselves and with the protection of anonymity. A random sample would not be likely to produce more reliable results: and certainly they would not have been as detailed.

An element of apparent inconsistency in the bishops' reasoning process is that the Kennedy-Heckler study was a random sample and was carefully designed to include priests of a number of different categories—including a wide spectrum of age groupings and both diocesan and religious order priests. Although the American bishops commissioned this study, they seem no happier with these results, and it is no longer available from their literature distribution center, the National Conference of Catholic Bishops in Washington, DC.

My personal reaction to Richard Sipe's book, the predominately black cover of which is suggestive of funerals, was that the detached clinical language he uses tends to have the opposite effect: that of emphasizing the pain and sense of entrapment that must have been part of the lives of so many he interviewed. Though the women involved were not contacted directly, their pain and frustration also deserve acknowledgment—many were caught in long-term relationships with men who refused to commit to marriage. (To reply that they consented to the status quo in all cases would be simplistic; it is in the nature of love to be hopeful). But not everyone is able to muster the courage and energy required to get out of a spiritually destructive situation, especially when they may be educationally unprepared for anything else and there are concerns about how the rent is going to get paid.

In both studies there also seem to have been many who expressed a profound psychological attachment to the role of priest. The Kennedy-Heckler study offers precise documentation of this. (This is not to question the sacrament of Holy Orders, but it is also a reality that sometimes people are forced to leave irredeemably destructive marriages—and marriage also is a sacrament—even though married people tend not to define their personal identity in terms of their marital status.) Once at a CORPUS meeting I heard a member say bluntly, "I left the priesthood to save my soul." One wonders if there have been others less fortunate!

The chapter in Richard Sipe's book that I found the most disturbing was entitled, "The Masturbations." The text and words of the priests interviewed communicated a piercing and oppressive loneliness. A sense of the truly dreadful was evoked that was all the more powerful because it was apparently unconscious. It is said of Abraham Lincoln that years before becoming president he once witnessed a slave auction, at which he was led to exclaim, "If I ever get a chance to hit this thing, I'm going to hit it hard." Ecclesiastical bureaucrats need occasionally to be reminded that there are people out there: on the other side of all those regulations. Nor should we forget Christ's admonition regarding the scribes and Pharisees: "They tie up heavy burdens and lay them on men's shoulders, but will they lift a finger to move them? Not they!"[53] Along with the pain, the hypocrisy of all this is obvious.

A prominent negative feature of bureaucratic and hierarchical organizations (and there are also some positive features) is that they enable the individual to avoid a sense of personal responsibility for problems. Thus in the Catholic Church there is a tendency to blame the Pope for everything. While this attitude is partially reality-based, it is also partially a cop-out. The traditional docility of the Catholic lay person is in danger of crossing the line into actual indifference. The general attitude, facilitated by the structure of the Church—that it's the responsibility of the priest, the bishop or *il papa* to fix things—is combined with a sense that they aren't really listening. Such defeatism is not completely justified; lay people are in the best position to initiate the change process and this has actually occurred in the past.

The incidents of sexual abuse of children by priests seem to be increasing in frequency and they have become the focus of much negative and embarrassing publicity for the Church—and even the subject of a 1990 movie, "Judgment," starring Keith Carradine. In 1985 there were 30 cases of priests involving at least 100 children which had reached the public courts—totalling some $400,000,000 in damages from the Church if all cases had been upheld.[54]

---

[53] Matthew 23:4.
[54] Sipe, p. 184.

In June 1985 the *National Catholic Reporter* reported that the cost of liability insurance to cover the possible sexual offenses of the clergy is becoming so prohibitively expensive for many dioceses that it may result in the denial of insurance coverage to the Catholic Church for such claims: a policy already adopted by the insurance industry for members of the psychiatric and psychological professions. These policy changes could threaten the very economic survival of the Church and seriously damage its ability to assist the poor and needy.

Another salient fact about pedophiles is that the rate of recurrence is high and is twice as high for those who prefer juveniles of the same sex.[55] The Church claims a high percentage of success for its treatment centers for wayward priests, but even one case of recurrence is too many. None of the Protestant churches feels the need to have such treatment centers to preclude the ongoing scandals that continue to proliferate within the Catholic Church. The aberrant Jimmy Bakers tend to be already marginalized from the mainline churches. This section of the book was first written in the fall of 1990, and since then the scandals have continued. A notable example is the allegations of a long-term pattern of juvenile sexual abuse that have been made against Joseph Ferrario, the bishop of Honolulu. And the financial damage to the Church because of costly lawsuits and settlements is proceeding at an alarming rate.[56]

---

[55] Sipe, p. 181.

[56] *Time,* August 19, 1991, p. 51.

It is not a coincidence, when one considers the etiology of most pedophilia, that a number of pedophiles have become priests. These persons usually have an immature level of psychosexual development and the prospect of sexual expression with an adult is frightening to them.[57] Many pedophiles also display a great need to maintain control in their relationships with others. Sipe has observed—and this may have a major bearing on the potential effectiveness of the Church's efforts to deal with these problems—that many seminarians begin studies for the priesthood in a state of psychosexual immaturity[58] and many are not even certain what their sexual orientation is.

Subjects in the Kennedy-Heckler study also repeatedly demonstrated the lack of a clear sense of gender identity.[59] This immaturity or lack of self-awareness is especially likely to be true of pedophiles. In turn the structured, supervised world of the seminary aids the psychological defense mechanisms of repression and denial. What can be ignored or pushed out of conscious awareness while involved in intellectual pursuits—with the goal of ordination—has a way of erupting later in the stressful, less organized environment that is the priesthood today. Sipe notes that "few pedophiles act out extensively prior to [ordination]."

The Vatican's new directives, which essentially call for closer supervision of seminarians regarding their

---

[57] *Abnormal Psychology and Modern Life,* p. 400.

[58] p. 162.

[59] pp. 11-12.

sexual orientation and ability to remain sexually abstinent as well as for prohibiting priests from leading any
sort of double life, don't really address the human ability
to repress and hide unacceptable tendencies even from
the self.

From a base figure of 20 percent homosexuality in the
period of 1960-1980, Sipe estimates that the incidence
among priests has increased in the last decade from 38
percent to as high as 50 percent in some areas.[60] These
estimates are from sources he considers reliable and the
statistics from those suffering and dying from AIDS
would certainly seem to bear out this claim. Many lay
people in the Catholic Church are of the opinion that
homosexuality among the Catholic clergy is increasing. It
should not be surprising, considering the human tendency to make a virtue of necessity, that homosexuals are
attracted into the priesthood in disproportionate numbers. One priest even told Sipe, "If I'm homosexual, I
might as well serve the Church." As in pedophilia, it is
possible to control or deny a homosexual orientation
during seminary training, but the self-imposed discipline
can more easily break down later.

From the preceding, one can conclude that by its
disproportionate emphasis on marital status or the
willingness to remain single as a qualification for priesthood, the Catholic Church is providing a haven for the
sexually defiant or psychologically immature.[61]

---

[60] p. 107.
[61] *Time,* September 24, 1990, p. 79.

Though there are still some fine men who choose the Catholic priesthood from the highest of motives, the emphasis on the acceptance of celibacy also attracts another form of immaturity—the rigid or rule-oriented personality—who also seems to be entering the priesthood in disproportionate numbers. Jesus confirmed a number of rules and gave them a foundation in charity or the good of society—including those for sexual conduct—but he condemned the scribes and the Pharisees for their multiplication of and emphasis upon human regulations.

The widespread Catholic educational program for Confraternity of Christian Doctrine (CCD) instructors makes the point that the person who acts mainly from rules or fear of punishment is an immature personality type. Sipe refers to these priests as:

> hardworking and devoted and willing to sacrifice everything, but oftentimes exhibiting a rigidity in their lives and relationships. They are men of the letter and are, accordingly, valuable lieutenants in the clerical army because of their devotion to detail, rules and order. . . . Their inflexibility can be construed as conviction.[62]

Is what can be viewed as the Church's stubborn rigidity in continuing to insist upon celibacy in the years following Vatican II leading to a revival of this personality type? A 1989 article entitled "New Priests" that appeared in a Catholic magazine would suggest an

---

[62] p. 91.

affirmative answer. The cover of the publication showed a basically handsome young priest or seminarian who was, however, scowling and in a defensive posture, his arms folded protectively across his chest. The content of the article made clear that many new priests are heavily into rules and specific devotions and some even favor a return to the Latin Mass.

Such rigid people often have a tendency to be self-righteous as well, as the following incident illustrates. After Mass one Sunday, I spoke with the seminarian assigned to the church I was attending. He was also a convert from a Protestant denomination, and I wanted to ask how his father, who was seriously ill, felt about his becoming a priest. The seminarian replied that his father's feelings were mixed. The topic of celibacy arose, and I expressed my belief that the Holy Spirit was leading the Church in another direction. I also stated that loneliness and burnout were frequent problems of priests (he agreed) and without getting specific, asked the young man if he were aware of the problems three consecutive pastors at a nearby parish had experienced (This will be discussed in the following section; there was one early death; a case of alcoholism and another of burnout and mental aberrations). The seminarian responded that he personally "wasn't ready to let go of celibacy," and "they (the pastors) just weren't the right people." With this sort of attitude, it is virtually guaranteed that this young man will encounter some type of serious difficulty in his years as a priest.

The attraction of a rule-oriented personality to the priesthood has inescapable pastoral ramifications. Such persons when placed in leadership positions naturally attract other kindred spirits and soon the entire character of a parish is affected. One such pastor I know was vociferous in claiming that Vatican II was a mistake that had "emptied the churches." Since the Protestants are having an equally hard time filling their pews, I could not help but wonder how much emptier Catholic pews might be if Latin—and missal juggling—had been preserved for posterity. No wonder this pastor's congregation was factionalized with one group even emphasizing salvation by works alone—which is of course a heresy. There was a corresponding neglect of charity among parishioners, the "weightier things" of which Jesus spoke.[63]

In fairness it should be pointed out that this pastor appears to have a basically healthy personality structure; this emerging rigidity might be regarded as an occupational hazard—caused at least in part by the absence of a spouse and children who might have served as a softening influence or to present alternative viewpoints. Like many other priests who choose to remain, in my opinion this man was authentically called to priesthood but not to celibacy. Sexual temptations are not always a serious problem for priests in this category; rather, their singleness seems to have the effect of impoverishing their personalities and their ministries to others.

By denying the potentially valuable contribution that the pastor's spouse might make to a congregation and by its insistence on celibacy the Catholic Church as a whole

---

[63]   Matthew 23:23.

is thus impoverishing itself. When the willingness to remain unmarried becomes a focus of the vocation approval process, the Church's ability to choose the best qualified candidates for the priesthood is impaired. The people are poorly served by clergy with handicaps—who may burn out, die early or create a scandal. If the ordination of marrieds were permitted, the Catholic Church would not only have more applicants for ordination but would also be able to be more selective.

The World Synod of Bishops in the fall of 1990 approved some specific proposals designed to improve the selection and education of candidates for the priesthood, including mandatory psychological testing. Dr. Harry Olson, a Baltimore psychologist who has administered similar tests to Lutheran seminary candidates, says this is not a panacea for although a modern battery of tests is quite successful in identifying problem personalities—such as those prone to anger and excessive rigidity—still the tests are not designed to detect sexual aberrations such as homosexuality or pedophilia. It remains quite possible for such persons to slip through undetected by standard procedures, especially when those tested may not be fully self-aware. Dr. Olson also observed that a rule like mandatory celibacy tends to attract problem personalities, specifically "neurotics". Should a test battery successfully weed such aberrants out, the question arises as to how many candidates would be left.

Unfortunately the spiritual authority of the Catholic Church is eroded when the Church is widely regarded as incapable of grappling with current issues or responding to problems that have the potential to destroy its credibility. And the scandals do scandalize.

The secular media often seem to have an agenda that is at odds with Christianity. Yet truth is where you find it and in the celibacy rule—with its shaky historical and theological underpinnings and immensely damaging results—the media have spotted a substantive problem that threatens to destroy the Catholic Church.

Even if the Catholic Church is not irretrievably changed by lack of priests, it is in danger of being symbolically ghettoized and ignored by an increasingly secular society as is demonstrated by the negative publicity generated by the celibacy question on popular TV programs such as "Geraldo" and "Donahue". Unfortunately what is seen by many as the Catholic Church's hypocrisy and unwillingness to change on celibacy is used as justification for ignoring its teachings on everything.

To summarize: we as a Church and the hierarchy specifically are guilty of giving bad example and neglecting to project into the future. Within 50 years, if change is not forthcoming, the majority of Catholic churches could be without a priest and the damage caused by scandals, defections, and financially costly lawsuits is progressing at a much more rapid rate.

Questions for discussion or consideration:

1) Have you observed any damaging effects of celibacy personally in your parish or the Church?

2) Have you been involved in situations or discussions in which, because of its insistence on mandatory celibacy, the Church has been ridiculed?

3) The Catholic Church is the oldest institution in the Western world, but bureaucracies tend to make decisions without consulting the knowledge base of other disciplines, such as sociology and psychology. Can you recall some instances of this kind of decision-making?

3

Psycholgical and ◆ Physical Health Issues Related to Mandatory Celibacy

"It is not good for man to be alone" (Genesis 2:18).

The reality of priestly life today is that many, if not most, Catholic priests are lacking in close personal relationships. They are often also without an effective support system, especially if they have no family members living nearby or are not members of a religious community—which can function as a sort of substitute family giving structure, identity and some degree of emotional support. However, because of the diminishing populations in many religious orders, an increasing number of these priests are finding themselves placed in assignments where they do not live in community.

Current data from both science and medicine strongly documents the necessity of having some psychologically intimate relationships if both mental and physical health are to be maintained. Even the bishops are discussing this and admit: "It is widely recognized today how important human closeness is to emotional vitality and a good self-image."[64] There is a biological basis for our need to form loving, human relationships and if we fail to fulfill that need, our health is in peril.[65]

But the bishops also acknowledge that the attainment of interpersonal closeness is made more difficult by the celibate commitment and the tension it imposes between distance and closeness.[66] Friendships with other males, even other priests, are often superficial and revolve around activities such as sports. There is frequently no real sharing of feelings or problems—that's not the accepted way of doing things among men in our society.

A preponderance of men in the United States report that they have no close relationships with members of the same sex. My 13-plus years as a marriage counsellor substantiate this peculiarity as well. A man's colleagues are perceived as potential competitors—and this tends to hold true, in an offbeat kind of way, for those in clerical circles as well. Too much self-disclosure is not considered masculine and is even equated with a loss of face. Too much closeness raises the specter of homosexuality. Atlanta psychologist Augustus Napier reports on "two doctors whose lockers were next to each other in the surgical dressing room of a hospital. For years they

---

[64] The Bishops' Committee on Priestly Life and Ministry, "The Priest and Stress," p. 11.
[65] James Lynch, *The Broken Heart: the Medical Consequences of Loneliness*, p. 1.
[66] "The Priest and Stress," p. 10.

talked about sports, money and other safe 'male' subjects. Then one of them learned that the other had tried to commit suicide and never so much as mentioned the attempt to him. So much for male bonding."[67]

The Kennedy-Heckler study reported that almost an identifying characteristic of the largest subgroup of Catholic priests studied (the underdeveloped) was the absence of close friendships—in many cases combined with a personal uneasiness about intimacy.[68] Priests who share a rectory are usually (but not always) cordial, but a certain distance is observed.

Sipe's research mentions this as well. Yet if exhaustion, burnout and other stress-related problems are to be avoided, Catholic priests need comfortable relationships in which they can just be themselves and where others will relate to them as human beings and not merely in their ministerial role. Such relationships are often difficult to find within one's parish community where the congregants tend to project their own images onto the clergy and not see them as they are.[69]

The priest's efforts to seek friendship in nonclerical circles are often subject to misinterpretation, loss or built-in limitations. There is also the possibility, in the case of a friendship with a married couple for example, that the priest will be viewed by other parishioners as guilty of favoritism. The older the Catholic priest gets, the more his non-priestly contemporaries and siblings are

[67] *Time,* fall 1990 Special Issue: "Women: The Road Ahead."
[68] p. 9.
[69] John Sanford, *Ministry Burnout,* p. 43.

enmeshed in their own families—which begins a subtle distancing of the priest from those who have heretofore been his support community.

Then there are those Catholic priests who try to develop nonsexual friendships with women in their community. This is often subject to misinterpretation, and the artificial limitations or barriers that must be observed sometimes involve such strain that the effort tends to be seen as too difficult. Experimentation with such relationships was popular among clerical circles in the 1970s and called "the third way"[70] but most such attempts have been largely abandoned as being too treacherous or troublesome.

If all these possible solutions to the problem of achieving intimacy outside of marriage or community are, to one degree or another, unsatisfactory or unworkable, then the Catholic Church, with its continuing insistence on forced singleness, finds itself faced with an extremely uncomfortable dilemma. If "human closeness" is essential to health, how can this be achieved within a structure that does not permit marriage? Of course not all marriages are ideal and many today end in divorce, but this does not preclude the fact that marriage and family are still the most dependable sources of emotional intimacy and support.

The nature of loneliness, which is becoming endemic in our society, and the predicament its resolution poses for Catholic priests, can be clarified by some examination

---

[70] Sipe, pp. 98-99.

of the phenomenon of falling in love. As anyone who has had this powerful experience can report, although there is a sexual component, mainly this is mental and emotional. Many single people are lonely to some degree. When they discover someone who takes this sense of isolation away and with whom there can be "a meeting of the minds," an attachment develops. "This one, at last, is bone of my bones and flesh of my flesh."[71]

To have to abandon or leave a person with whom one has fallen in love is extremely difficult and may be impossible without sustaining psychological damage. At the least the sense surfaces that life will never again be the same. The language used to refer to this phenomenon ("falling") correctly suggests that it can be involuntary, at least in part.

Several years ago the television program "60 Minutes" did a story on a Catholic priest in an isolated parish in Montana who had the misfortune (as defined by the Church) of falling in love. When he reported this and his subsequent marriage to his congregation, he was met with applause! "All the world loves a lover." His congregation were pleased with him in general and asked his superiors that he be allowed to remain, but he was forced to resign.

In this case, the maintenance of the institutional rule of celibacy took precedence over the will of the people—and perhaps over their welfare as well. The forced resignation of a popular priest whose performance was

---

[71] Genesis 2:23.

apparently superior tends to leave a bad taste in the mouth of the congregation, who never again will trust the system in the same way and will always be wary of any replacements sent to the church. A difficult situation could also have been created for the priest's replacement, if any.

For the priest who resigns in mid-life or later, a major reason—and there are often others—is usually that he has formed an attachment to a particular woman and has a desire for family life and children, not that he is incapable of controlling his sexual drive. By this age many priests realize that the ministry will not compensate for living alone—and, even worse, contemplating old age and dying alone.

The lack of a close relationship with whom to share thoughts and feelings can also lead to a gamut of psychological dysfunctions, including depression. Sometimes it is possible to block off painful feelings such as anxiety or loneliness from conscious awareness through frenetic activity or hide such sorrow beneath a smile. Such individuals literally do not know how they feel, but their feelings are reflected in measurable physical symptoms such as hypertension; blood pressure becomes measurably elevated when certain topics are discussed, even without conscious awareness of distress.[72]

What implications does this have for the health of the priest who often has to deal with upsetting situations—

---

[72] James Lynch, *The Language of the Heart: The Body's Response to Human Dialog,* p. 237.

the traumas, sicknesses and deaths in the parish as well as the accompanying negative emotions that go along with these. The overload of negatives that can occur during a long session in the confessional is another burden that a Catholic priest finds difficult to shed when he steps away—frequently to his own reality that he has no consistent or effective support system for himself.

Many long-term Catholic communities have seen a priest in their parish become consumed by loneliness. It is painful to watch the local pastor who has no apparent close relationships nearby, no family living in the area and whose friends have begun to die off or move away. It is no wonder such a priest often finds his difficulties compounding. "The Christmas blues" set in because he was alone for the holiday. A full-blown clinical depression of several months then developed, including sleep disturbances, neglect of personal appearance and neglect of all but essential (liturgical) duties. His depression was reported to his bishop, but what action, if any, was taken is unknown. About 18 months later, the depression seems to have been replaced by bizarre behavior including disappearing for a month without telling anyone where he was; refusing to hear confessions ("I'm tired of hearing sins"); and walking in the halls of the parish school mumbling to himself. He remains in a more or less permanent state of social withdrawal and has reduced his contacts with parish groups such as the Knights of Columbus and is seldom seen in the classroom.

His impaired judgment has affected his congregation in practical ways. They seriously need a new church building, but he decided to scrap the original design in favor of one that was too expensive. A third design was then produced, but the congregation became deeply divided over plans to finance the new building by selling some church property to a developer. The pastor was interviewed by a local newspaper and reported that he felt caught in a difficult situation as the congregation had outgrown the large multipurpose room, used for Sunday Mass. The priest's superiors are distantly supportive of his efforts, but the degree of support he receives on a day-to-day basis is doubtful. The obvious question is raised: If he had had a spouse and family to offer emotional support and advice, how much of these difficulties, both for himself and his congregation, might have been avoided?

The financial problems connected with the proposed new church have now been at least partially resolved, and there were plans for a ground breaking ceremony in the fall of 1991. But the truth is, it is difficult to heal divisions in the congregation once such problems arise.

Another syndrome that can sometimes result from long-term service to others is the "exhausted ego." In his book, *Ministry Burnout,* John Sanford points out that people need feedback not only to ascertain what aspects of the current situation can be changed and what are beyond our control, but also for reassurance of worth. "It is almost impossible to walk the spiritual path alone. At some point everyone needs a companion on the way,

someone with whom we can share openly and honest-
ly."[73] A paid therapist may sometimes be necessary,[74]
but this is often a case of closing the barn door after the
horse has escaped, for a therapist is not a family substitute or a permanent solution to the problem of loneliness.

Sanford also compares psychic energy to metabolic
energy—it is always being used up and must be replen-
ished.[75] It is difficult to overestimate the importance of
family life in this process; families make demands on us,
but they also refresh. Parent burnout can occur too, but
children are generally cheerful. A different sort of weari-
ness comes from dealing with the repetitive negative
situations that are often found in congregations. Also,
children are malleable, usually are not needy bottomless
pits and, unlike some adults, tend to repay the emotion
and time invested by growing up.

The circumstances of a priest's life and frequent lack
of psychological intimacy can also cause lesser forms of
disturbed functioning. Some priests are renowned for the
inappropriate affect of appearing at all times excessively
happy. The emerging eccentricity of a basically very good
priest in a nearby parish took this form. During a
Sunday sermon he mentioned an incident of sitting
outside a building where a wedding reception was being
held and seeing a beautiful sunset, at which he was led
to exclaim, "Thank you, Jesus!" This popular and es-

[73] p. 79.
[74] This suggestion is also made by the bishops in "The Priest and
Stress," p. 22.
[75] p. 104.

teemed priest was however beginning to get some strange looks from parishioners; he left on sabbatical shortly afterward.

The distant deference afforded priests by most members of their congregations is of no real help to them in their efforts to maintain adequate levels of reality testing; it can even be part of the problem. To maintain good mental health, the cleric must cultivate ordinary relationships which help guard against egocentricity (a particular danger for celibate clergy especially since a spouse and children have a way of bringing people down to earth) and becoming lost in one's public *persona*.[76] The clergyman who falls into this trap can lose sight of who he really is; his ability to interpret and respond to reality can be correspondingly impaired. There is also the tendency to ignore the advice of others since they feel that they have special access to truth. An example is that of a bishop who visited another local church and with whom I spoke (and I think courteously) about a perceived lack of effective support for the prolife movement. I also gave some suggestions, based on experience and the advice of others. He listened politely, but it was apparent his mind was already made up: "*I* (his emphasis) decide what we're going to do." He has since decided to seek advice and form coalitions on other issues, but the Baltimore archdiocese's lack of support for prolife candidates—which could have been done legally by emphasizing issues rather than specific candidates—has done consider-

[76]   Ibid., pp. 44-45, 76.

able damage to the prolife cause in Maryland. There were four notable losses by such candidates in November, 1990.

The importance of maintaining a daily prayer life and making an annual spiritual retreat in avoiding the destructive effects of stress is mentioned several times in the bishops' document.[77] I have no reason to believe any of these men neglected personal prayer, but it does not seem to have avoided these negative effects of a life-style that can only be described as pathological.

A related psychological problem with manifestations familiar to many parishioners—though they often have difficulty defining it precisely or identifying causes—is that many priests are seduced into the abuse of the power they possess in parish life and as those in charge of specific ministries. Power becomes in effect a substitute for family life; it can also be an alternative way of affirming the priest's masculinity. Sipe quotes the saying that "power is the lust of the clergy."[78] He also quotes a speech by Fr. Andrew Greely, sociologist and popular author: "[Some clergy] are so caught up in the game of ecclesiastical power that they transfer their urge for pleasure to that all-consuming game." Eugene Kennedy is quoted in a 1986 article in the *National Catholic Reporter* as saying: "The gratification experienced from this asexual mode of functioning (using power to dominate

[77] "The Priest and Stress," p. 22.
[78] p. 84.

others) is in some sense a substitute for mature sexual gratification."

Most parishioners in the Catholic Church have had unfortunate experience with a new priest who quickly evidences a capricious, unpredictable quality to decision-making. Existing programs are sometimes summarily dismantled or lay leadership ignored, protests notwithstanding, because the priest appears to be on a power trip. Such priests are not bad people, but having no one to counter their whims, they fall into well-intentioned, but insensitive decision-making and often are unaware of their own internal dynamics.

During my years as a song leader I shifted from an attitude of friendliness to new priests to one of fear and trembling. One new priest decided, and without consulting lay leaders, to change radically the existing music program. The same priest was placed in charge of the Eucharistic ministers of the parish. Despite protests, he decreed that one of my friends, an epileptic on disability who was subject to *grand mal* seizures and also suffered from phlebitis, wasn't sick enough to receive Communion at home. (It should be noted that this person had made himself a bit of a nuisance, but had always had a good relationship with the Eucharistic minister assigned to him.) My friend died suddenly about a year late without receiving the Sacraments. I have no real doubts about his salvation, but it would have been appropriate if he had been able to receive Communion during the week of his death.

This power ingredient which is related to forced celibacy is also seen in the hierarchy for the appetite for power can be corporate as well as individual. Other institutions in our society—big business and big government as well as Big Church (and the Catholic Church is the largest Christian denomination in the U.S.)—tend to be wary of the family because it prevents them from having total control over the individual. Such secular entities as IBM ("I've Been Moved") routinely are accused of fomenting antifamily policies. Yet this is not necessary to success. Businesses and denominations around the country have successfully integrated marriage and ministry.

An interesting case could also be made that the Church's antifamily policies conflict with the civil or constitutional rights enjoyed by American citizens which include the right to marry, within limitations prescribed by the individual states. And unlike some positions the Church has taken (its opposition to premarital sex and abortion, for example) its prohibition of marriage to its clergy is without a clear religious or Scriptural mandate. The Roman Catholic Church is the only Christian denomination that continues to forbid a married clergy.

One consideration in the hierarchy's reluctance to confront the need for change is a certain sense that a predominately married clergy might somehow undermine legitimate authority within the Church. But history and the experience of other denominations offer no clear evidence of this. The celibacy requirement was one reason leading to the Orthodox-Catholic split, but these denominations have been relatively stable since. Without exception, the most conservative Protestant churches permit a married clergy.

Rather than undermining Church authority, a change in this celibacy rule might actually help to legitimize it. A degree of flexibility in nonessentials is indispensable in maintaining all long-term relationships—between groups as well as individuals. Studies have shown that job satisfaction, combined with a sense that employers have some concern for their employees as human beings, is a more effective inducement to worker productivity than salary.

The employer-employee relationship is not an exact parallel to the relationship between a priest and bishop, of course, but it offers some usable lessons. The gospels speak clearly to the question of what is effective leadership. Jesus said he came "not to be served, but to serve," and followed his words by a startling example: washing his disciples' feet.[79]

The problem of psychological burnout among those in the helping professions makes Catholic priests prime candidates for this both because of their lack of family support and the sporadic but never-ending input of other people's problems. One of the main identifying features of burnout is a decreased tolerance—sometimes following years of ability to maintain a certain distance—for the physical or emotional pain of others. The helping person's emotional filter breaks, so to speak, and a lot of pain outside becomes internalized. I had personal experience with this syndrome during my years as a social worker in a Maryland state hospital and was ultimately forced to

[79]   John 13:14-15.

resign. Going home to an empty house at the end of a difficult day was also a factor in the accumulation of my stress. A priest of many years shortly before his retirement was heard to mention in passing (a comment representing "systems overflow" rather than a deliberate wish to confide) that when talking to people he sometimes felt "bounced from one emotion to another."

Unusual outbursts of anger can also be symptoms of burnout. This priest was also developing a reputation for a sort of free-floating hostility. Chronic tiredness, depression and boredom can also be indications of burnout—which is both a recently identified syndrome and one that is becoming endemic in our society.[80]

In addition to dealing with other people's problems constantly and the negatives in our communities, clergy must deal with other factors leading to burnout—the repetitive nature of much of their work combined frequently with a lack of observable results.[81] Often there is an absence of clear standards to measure success and failure, so priests feel they must constantly live up to the expectations of others. With the increasing clergy shortage, overwork alone can cause burnout. A few years ago, another priest of my acquaintance was promoted to pastor of a large city parish. About two years later, his conversation and correspondence (a note my mother received from him in response to a contribution) were becoming disjointed, as if he were in danger of a break-

---

80   Sanford, pp. 1, 3.
81   Ibid., pp. 6-7.

down. The note mentioned overwork and "clergy short-age," but in general he is not one to complain. When asked earlier how his new assignment was going, he simply replied that it was "a challenge." Even if he manages to maintain his sanity, it seems unlikely that he will attain a normal life span.

Rapid changes in the expected role of a priest—for example, from the authoritarian to consensus styles of leadership—create confusion as it is impossible to meet all demands and expectations. There are just too many meetings and the shortage also prevents many priests from being able to specialize in what they do best. In addition to all this—and this is clearly related to their single state—Catholic priests tend to worry about their retirement years![82]

The family's ability to offer financial help to its members should not be undervalued, but in addition to providing emotional support and personal affirmation, in a very practical way, families can help their members who are clergy avoid exhaustion by scheduling their time. This is demonstrated repeatedly in the lives of Protestant clergy I know who are encouraged by their families to take care of themselves and to reserve time for family recreation.

Since there is a growing expectation that all priests should take a weekly day off anyway,[83] why can't they have a family with whom to spend it? Vacations and

---

[82] "The Priest and Stress", pp. 3, 6.
[83] Ibid., p. 21.

"time off for literary and cultural pursuits" are also mentioned by the bishops as preventives of burnout, but the question of how the conscientious priest is to make use of them in an era of increasing numbers of Catholics and fewer priests to serve them remains unanswered. A significant reality is that once a priest becomes a bishop, the Church's middle management level, the danger of burnout is decreased. Though bishops have problems of a different nature—financial, administrative and dealing with the public—the negative input they receive from immediate personal sources—such as sins and funerals—is reduced. The plight of the priest at the parish level is not an urgent concern for most bishops, though they can intellectualize about it, because they are no longer personally affected by it.

The attitude of the hierarchy of "that's how we've always done things" and its messy psychological ramifications is probably a greater barrier to change than the dubious theological props now in place. When a position is taken ("My mind is made up, don't confuse me with facts") an effort is made to bend reality to support the preconceived idea and to ignore facts that don't support it.

Bishops are understandably reluctant to confront this issue on a human level and no one wants to make the first move, though there have been some individual bishops courageous enough to speak out. The issue of celibacy is a source of personal uneasiness because it not only calls for what might be an uncomfortable degree of introspection, but it brings the whole role of chastity (obeying the celibate promise) to an open (read, awkward) forum. Of course there are some who are personally called to the celibate life, but many others struggle with chastity.

In the final chapters of his book, Richard Sipe criticizes the Church for requiring celibacy but not doing enough to support it. Seminarians are not taught how to achieve a positive celibacy, and the issue is much wider than the absence of sexual expression. In fact, organized information on this vital topic is lacking. Those who have had personal experience in achieving a happy, single life are not sought out so they could share how they have accomplished this. From personal experience, I can report that the achievement of a happy single life becomes attainable when something is found in the way of accomplishment or self-expression that is capable of compensating for what has been lost. But this is difficult for the priest, as the institutional Church imposes additional constraints. Ordinarily a priest may not adopt children, own a home or engage in certain political or social involvements. A priest cannot even play the organ and simultaneously offer Mass; I know a gifted organist who was ordained several years ago. One local priest, Father Joe Breighner, left parish work to found the Pastoral Counselling Centers. He also has a weekly radio program in which he discusses a wide range of social, personal and theological issues in his unique poetic style. But for most priests, the result of ordination is a severely constricted life after the "highs" of preaching and first Mass have worn off.

One recovering alcoholic pastor admitted to the congregation in a sermon that not long after his ordination he felt as if he were marooned. While his friends were having children and enjoying visible forms of success, "there (he) was, a priest."

This is not to devalue the *infinite* value of the Mass and the Sacraments, but to maintain our mental health, most of us need more visible evidence of achievement or at least the awareness of having contributed to the welfare of those who will come after us. Generativity is the task of mid-life.

Jesus compares his kingdom to the "pearl of great price"[84] and calls his disciples to demonstrate a willingness to sacrifice everything—if that is the calling. But as a matter of practicality, few are called to actual asceticism or given the gift of contemplative prayer.

In a strange sort of way, the Church's insistence on celibacy sometimes contributes to mediocrity in the priesthood or to a sort of passive-aggressive attitude. Many priests seem to be operating on the premise that having already made the ultimate sacrifice, the quality of their ministries from then on is a secondary issue. There are, of course, many priests who put forth their best efforts, but the lack of feedback from others—that is often a side effect of celibacy since fellow priests are understandably reluctant to criticize their colleagues—is a significant handicap.

Much anecdotal and personal observation of the priesthood has been given validation by research. The previously mentioned Kennedy-Heckler study of the psychological development of American priests published

---

[84] Matthew 13:45-46.

in 1971 was commissioned by the bishops of the United States who voted to conduct such an assessment. This study included both clinical interviews and psychological tests from 271 respondents. The study design was exact and the total number reflected a random sample with simultaneous and appropriate representation from all parts of the country, all major subgroups, age categories and both diocesan (secular) and order priests.

The results of the study tended to separate the subjects into four subgroups: the psychologically underdeveloped, representing 57 percent of the priests studied; the developing, which were 29 percent; the maldeveloped, which were eight percent; and the developed, which were six percent of the total number. Criteria used to assess psychological development included the quality of relationships with others and degree of comfort with the self—all issues of personal identity and self-expression.

The largest group of priests—the underdeveloped—manifested their lack of growth chiefly in their relationships with other people—which were characterized by a lack of intimacy and were frequently distant, highly stylized and unrewarding. Some of these difficulties with closeness were caused at least partially by unresolved difficulties with identity formation. Many tended to identify themselves through their role of priesthood rather than through their own personalities. A large percentage of these underdeveloped had not completely achieved sexual identity—in effect they had not fully resolved the developmental tasks of adolescence. Many used disproportionate amounts of psychological energy to control their conflicts and prevent their public behavior from going out of bounds.[85]

The next largest category of priests—the developing—were intent on establishing greater closeness with others. The effort toward growth was often precipitated by some significant life change or crisis, such as a new work assignment or the death of parents, with subsequent awareness of isolation and loneliness. A high degree of introspection and a setting aside of defense mechanisms attended the growth process. This was also sometimes initiated by a spiritual experience or a relationship with a woman—which sometimes brought "a kind of value and quality of experience never known before."[86]

The challenge of finding that there is more to life than was suspected sometimes led these priests to reconsider their vocational commitments and their total ideas of faith, priesthood and Church. In other words, those in the psychologically developing category were the most likely to leave the active priesthood. "The developing person seriously questions celibacy because . . . he has a new appreciation of the values of love and human relationships," not usually because of a wish toward rebellion for its own sake.[87]

A few years after completing the study, Eugene Kennedy also left the active priesthood. He married several years later.

[85]   pp. 9, 11-13.
[86]   pp. 144, 147.
[87]   pp. 156, 158.

The third category of priests—the maldeveloped—were characterized by a sometimes pathological use of defense mechanisms to deal with their feelings, which they were unable to handle directly.[88] Negative feelings about the self, sexual identity problems, feelings of hostility and difficulty in dealing with authority figures were found in this group. Since this study was published almost 20 years ago, one could suspect that if it were replicated today in our much-changed culture, the figure of eight percent for this group might be somewhat higher, as might be the figure of 57 percent for the underdeveloped group.

The fourth and smallest category of priests—the psychologically developed—were characterized by an acceptance of their own individuality and personalities combined with more positive relationships with others. This group also had the ability to be appropriately dependent or independent and were characterized by a strong religious commitment and prayer life and the ability to work productively—usually in situations that suited their individual abilities. These priests also tended to have firm sexual identities and an acceptance of themselves as sexual beings—even while in most cases respecting their celibate commitments.[89] It seems likely that the priests in this group were personally called to celibacy or the Evangelical Counsels. One productive and reasonably

[88] p. 72.
[89] pp. 175-187.

well-integrated superior of a religious community is cited in particular.

The Kennedy-Heckler study stressed that the priest-hood itself is a valuable vocation, but that the institutionally created constraints create a problem. The study concludes that the effect of these strictures is twofold: to attract into the priesthood a disproportionate number of underdeveloped people and to "reward and enhance lack of development," for the rule of celibacy tends to reinforce specific aspects of psychological underdevelopment.[90]

As has been observed by others, by continuing its present policies, the Church is suffering an enormous "brain drain" and is losing many of its most creative and emotionally integrated priests. These individuals have the potential of providing both effective spiritual leadership while being positive role models in the congregation—just as do many Christian clergy in other denominations.

Beyond this, it has been known for several years that the length of life as well as its quality can be affected by marital status and the painful experience of loneliness, a point made strongly and supported by statistical evidence in James Lynch's first book, *The Broken Heart: the Medical Consequences of Loneliness.*

The mortality statistics among those adult Americans who are not married are striking—a death rate from heart disease that is as much as two to five times

[90] pp. 13-14.

higher for unmarried individuals, including those who are divorced, widowed or single than for married Americans.[91]

Not only heart disease, but all causes of death in our country are consistently higher for divorced, single and widowed people of both sexes and all races; this tendency is especially pronounced among males—a fact long recognized by the actuarial tables of insurance companies.[92] Single people also consume more alcohol, with correspondingly high death rates from cirrhosis of the liver.

The Old Testament speaks directly of the increased vulnerability to life's misfortunes of the lonely and those who are without close ties to others: "Woe to the solitary man! For if he should fall, he has no one to lift him up. . . . Where a lone man may be overcome, two together can resist. A three-ply cord is not easily broken."[93]

The Book of Sirach also speaks of the positive correlation between marriage and both happiness and longevity: "Happy the husband of a good wife, twice lengthened are his days; a worthy wife brings joy to her husband, peaceful and full is his life. A good wife is a generous gift bestowed upon him who fears the Lord; be he rich or poor, his heart is content and a smile is ever on his face."[94]

[91] p. 35.
[92] pp. 38-39.
[93] Ecclesiastes 4:10, 12.
[94] 26:1-4.

The self-destructive life-styles of many single men, particularly, are a matter of common observation—and priests are not immune. Many Catholic congregations stand by helplessly as their priests proceed through life with "care-less" personal habits. I know a pastor of another church, a fine enthusiastic priest in his public *persona* who has does much to promote a positive spirit in his parish. However, he seems intent on killing himself with food and nicotine. A male acquaintance who has known the priest since childhood told me: "He doesn't take care of himself." Of course the prospect of a lonely retirement, especially for those who have no extended families with whom they feel welcome, does not help to promote good health habits.

There seem to be no statistics available on the longevity of Catholic priests vis-à-vis their clerical counterparts who are married with families, and the Catholic bishops admit a need for more information on this point. However, "The Priest and Stress" does mention that "neglecting his health can establish the priest in a coronary-prone way of life"[95] In recent years, there has been a rising number of early and sometimes sudden deaths among priests in the Baltimore area. A notable example is a former pastor of a nearby church (the one with the building controversy) who died in 1979 while participating in a soccer game. He had a congenital heart condition and had been warned by his physician against participating in sports, but told another priest about two

[95] p. 3.

years before his death that he had always led an active
life and didn't plan to change. However, a person who
basically wants to live *will* make life-style changes and
the inevitable question must be asked: did the priest
want to die? Or perhaps to put the situation more
accurately: he apparently had insufficient interest in
preserving his life. A parishioner accustomed to visiting
the rectory and talking with the priest, though not on a
deeply personal level, reported that he was overworked
and drinking heavily on occasion. However, he apparently
did not confide (or perhaps did not feel able to confide) in
friends, family or colleagues that he might have been
unhappy or experiencing problems. The "stiff upper lip"
is still expected as typical behavior in our society,
especially between males, but it does not lead to a long,
happy life. The person who has no spouse is frequently
also without a close friend, confidant and helper in life's
problems.

Lynch quotes a study done in 1961 at Massachusetts
General Hospital which involved patients—some of whom
were not apparently seriously ill—but all of whom were
lonely and isolated. These people were studied because
they had premonitions of imminent death and strangely
enough all died when they predicted they would. Lynch
concluded from this study that there is a unique will to
live in humans which is increased by closeness to other
people and decreased by loneliness.[96]

[96]   p. 152.

The two subsequent pastors at this church haven't fared much better. The first became an alcoholic, and the problems of the second have already been described. All three of these men seem to have found themselves essentially alone in facing life's difficulties, and both science and Scripture lead inevitably to the question: if they had been married, would the outcomes have been different?

The conclusion is inevitable that the Catholic Church's policy of forced singleness is contrary not only to Scriptural guidance but also to established truths in the fields of psychology and medicine. Mandatory celibacy too often becomes a formula for mandatory loneliness and its attendant problems. Though there is a place for self-sacrifice, even martyrdom, in the Christian life (and heroes of the faith like St. Maximilian Kolbe are recognized by the Catholic Church because while he was in a concentration camp, he offered his life in exchange for that of a married person with children) it should be remembered that the price has already been paid. Jesus established the priesthood as a means of bringing us to himself, but he is the Eternal High Priest:

> During the meal Jesus took bread, blessed it, broke it and gave it to his disciples. "Take this and eat it," he said, "this is My Body." Then he took a cup, gave thanks and gave it to them. "All of you must drink from it," he said, "for this is My Blood, the blood of the covenant, to be poured out in behalf of many for the forgiveness of sins."[97]

[97] Matthew 26:26-30.

Or as St. Paul puts it, "The law sets up as high priests men who are weak, but the word of the oath which came after the law appoints as priest the Son, made perfect forever."[98]

Questions for discussion or consideration:
1) By so far refusing to make changes and thereby neglecting the health of its priests, is the Catholic Church creating a class of sacrificial lambs?
2) How far is the view of the priest as expendable (he sometimes views himself in this way) created by the absence of a family?
3) How much is power a factor: power for its own sake—not power to accomplish a positive end—in the Church's reluctance to change its policies?

[98] Hebrews 7:28.

4

Celibacy and the ◆ People of God – Including Some Guidelines for Future Change

"Remain in him now, little ones so that when he reveals himself, we may be fully confident and not retreat in shame at his coming" (1 John 2:28).

A consequence of mandatory celibacy that has had profound impact on the development of Catholic theology has been an almost total rejection of the feminine. The devotion to the idealized figure of the Blessed Virgin is not a true exception, since the information Scripture provides on the mother of Christ is generalized rather than detailed.

Feminine influence, insights and modes of experiencing reality—which tend toward an integration of intellect with emotion and intuition together with a high degree of realism (what actually is, even when reality is painful)—have been largely ignored, often even held in contempt. Yet Scripture tells us, "Male and female he created them."[99] We recall that a woman, Mary Magdalene, was the first to see the risen Lord and that she received this gift while attempting to complete an unpleasant and probably dangerous task.

This repudiation of the feminine has been a major cause of the excessive intellectualization of theology and religious experience in the Catholic Church, though an occasional female mystic has been accepted. Men may not be inherently more cerebral than women, but it is surely no coincidence that intellectualization is one of the first-line defenses against instinctual drives[100] and one that has been demonstrably and effectively employed by those required to lead celibate lives.

The Kennedy-Heckler study documented that intellectualization was the psychological defense mechanism used most frequently by the largest group of priests—the underdeveloped—often as a defense against confronting painful emotions or issues of personal growth.[101]

In the development of Roman Catholic theology, there has been a related tendency toward theorizing, speculating and writing commentaries—and then commenting upon the commentaries—rather than returning to original sources. A current example of this is the ongoing debate about the relationship between Christ's human and divine natures—or at what point in his human life he realized his divinity. Some sources would fix this point of self-awareness at the Agony in the Garden or as late as

---

[99] Genesis 1:20.
[100] Anna Freud, *The Ego and the Mechanisms of Defense,* p. 160.
[101] p. 8.

the Crucifixion. Seemingly overlooked in such speculation are a number of Scripture texts such as Christ's early knowledge of his power to forgive sins;[102] the Transfiguration;[103] and the plain statement for those who have ears to hear: "Amen, amen, I say to you, before Abraham came to be, I Am."[104]

Doctrinal statements are at bottom a codification of actual experience; Christianity involves assent to that codification, but is fundamentally relational: friendship with a Person, not intellectual agreement with a formula or creed. The four gospels were all written during the first century A.D. and are basically straightforward first-person accounts, differing more in emphasis than in content. Even though Luke was not himself an eyewitness, he consulted with others who were.[105]

All four gospels relate the actual experience of a small group of people with their leader—who was however totally unique. When we contemplate the mind-blowing character of Ultimate Reality: that "he who dwells in unapproachable light" became one of us and that his main purpose in so doing was *to die in our place,* much of the theorizing that is called theology seems trivial.

This overly intellectual and logical theology created by the celibate tradition (when we consider what is known about psychological defense mechanisms, it seems improbable that this tradition could have developed in

102 Matthew 9:5-6.
103 "This is My beloved Son, listen to him" (Mark 9:7).
104 John 8:58.
105 Luke 1:1-2.

any other way), has helped to preserve doctrinal integrity. But, through its frequent separation of religious truth
from actual experience, faith difficulties for many have
also been created. It's time to move on.

John Cornwell's book, *A Thief in the Night: The
Mysterious Death of Pope John Paul I,* contains evidence
that this Pope who reigned for only 34 days might have
intended to make celibacy optional. Though he remained
a humble, unworldly man with an uncomplicated theology, John Paul's background was more academic than
pastoral and he was probably exposed to different
opinions on this law during his years of study.

Twice elected over his protests by the usual secret
ballot procedure, it was later disclosed that he had cast
his vote to Cardinal Aloisio Lorscheider of Fortaleza,
Brazil—a prelate who openly supported allowing a
married priesthood. One of the first requests made by
John Paul I after his election was for a consultation to be
arranged with some Orthodox clergy concerning the
theology of their Holy Orders.[106] It is very likely that
the celibacy law and perhaps its practical ramifications
would have been a topic of discussion at this gathering.

It also seems significant that this Pope's close friend
and confidante, Father Gennaro, left the active priesthood to marry after the Pope's death. It would also seem
very likely that John Paul and this priest who spent
considerable time together and used to go for walks,

---

[106] Cornwell, p. 310.

would have discussed the celibacy question, and perhaps Gennaro's feelings about it.

The conservatism of the next Pope, John Paul II, has benefitted the Church in important ways, for he has clearly enunciated the basic Christian truth during his peregrinations around the world. He has also worked assiduously to promote the Church's missionary effort, especially in Africa. However, this unconventional cleric who wrote his doctoral thesis on human sexuality has taken a consistently uncompromising position on celibacy—going so far as to order his bishops not even to communicate with groups advocating the ordination of married persons.

The potential danger this policy poses to Christian unity seems to have been overlooked. There are literally thousands of resigned priests who are prevented from serving the Church even though many of them still wish to remain as active clergy and/or are angry at what they perceive as unjust treatment.

Pope John Paul II has certainly been a help toward the peaceful liberation of much of Eastern Europe, and has promoted positive exchanges between the Church and the Communist world. However, he has refused even to discuss needed policy change within his own organization. There are of course some obvious and extreme dissimilarities between the Catholic Church and the Communist Party: for example, they are poles apart in ideology, and the Pope no longer has military might at his command. (Stalin once asked rhetorically, "How many divisions does the Pope have?") But events in the Soviet Union still offer some valuable lessons to the Church.

The will of the people, and their desire for greater democracy and control of their lives, is the ultimate irresistible force.

History demonstrates that leaders who refuse to lead will eventually be pushed out of the way. Unfortunately history also records that timing is of extreme importance, for if the call for freedom is disregarded, what occurs as pressures build up is not always positive. Chaos can result rather than true freedom. Action to create change before adverse conditions develop is the course greatly to be preferred—as opposed to damage control, mending fences or cleaning up a mess already made. In this sort of effort history also indicates that only limited success can be expected. For example, has France ever recovered completely from the French Revolution?

The crisis caused by celibacy is one of the most serious the Church has ever faced, and certainly the most serious since the Reformation. Ignoring scandals and disaffection, stonewalling and the use of power to suppress dissent were disastrous tactics then—and they aren't likely to be any more effective now. Or "is it necessary to destroy the city in order to save it?" The most dedicated proponents of clerical celibacy must ask themselves if this rule is really valuable enough to compensate for its potential destructiveness. What we have seen so far is not much more than the tip of the iceberg.

Historically, when there have been divisions in the Church, a precipitating factor has sometimes been a refusal by one or both parties to acknowledge the other. Withdrawing diplomatic recognition has been the *modus operandi.* Thus the papacy refused to talk with Martin Luther. The Lutheran-Catholic break may have been inevitable, but perhaps the level of animosity could have been reduced somewhat.

Most resigned priests remain loyal to the Roman Church, though they would like this rule to be changed, and a schism does not seem unavoidable. But ominous rumblings are being heard. If a split occurs because of a discipline rather than a doctrine, it would be doubly tragic.

An additional disquieting historical fact is that no previous division or schism has yet to be repaired. Dialogue is sometimes initiated centuries later—the current state of relations between the Roman and Anglican Churches being a case in point. This is an inauspicious time for such a break to occur because in our crisis-ridden era a negative and possibly lethal effect on the Church's Christian witness worldwide would be a likely consequence. Our increasingly secular world seems at times to be searching for ammunition to use against all Christian churches and for reasons to ignore Christ and his claims on their lives. The celibacy problem is currently being exploited by secular critics who ask, "Why should we take the Christians seriously when they can't even get their own personal problems solved any better than this?"

Should a schism over celibacy occur, its progress would likely be slow. But a snowball effect could be expected to follow as more and more Roman Catholic churches are left without a priest because of the rule of celibacy.

Currently CORPUS, also known as the Association for a Married Priesthood, is spreading rapidly worldwide with current chapters in many European and Latin American countries as well as in the United States. My association with the resigned priests' organization, and also some negative experiences in the process of writing this book and locating a publisher (it was refused by some Catholic publishers not because they disagreed with its contents, but because it wasn't sensational enough) have led me to a somewhat paradoxical conclusion. CORPUS may be the only group both seriously and realistically concerned about the future of the Catholic Church. Since many members have children, in many instances they have a greater sense of investment in the future than active clergy. Currently this group is working toward Church reform and they view a change to optional celibacy as an urgent priority.

Also high on the group's agenda is what is seen as a related issue—reform of the use of power within the Church. Though a clear majority would stop short of calling for the abolition of the papacy, many perceive a need for greater democracy within the Church so that the pope would return to his historical role within the Roman Church and be considered a sort of "first among equals", having perhaps a primary role as the arbiter of disagreements.

The Council of Jerusalem described in Acts 15 is an example; Peter, as the acknowledged leader, acted authoritatively (though he was supported by others) to eliminate circumcision and the Mosaic law as prerequisites to Christianity. Along with a predominately married priesthood, this less formal authority structure was characteristic of the early Church—and should be regarded as returning to our roots as Catholic Christians, not as something foreign or Protestant.

Following this New Testament model, national bishops' conferences or even individual bishops would be given more latitude to decide procedural questions (to call the celibacy rule a procedural matter might be to trivialize it, but it clearly fits into the category of rule rather than doctrine) in accord with the will and welfare of the people they serve. Such decisions should of course not be in conflict with the ultimate authority and general guidelines provided by Scripture.

The dichotomy between Church—or Church tradition—and Scripture that exists in the minds of many Protestants and even some Catholics, is an artificial one. It was the rudimentary organization of the first century Church that created the New Testament, not the reverse; this is a matter of historical record. For example, the Epistles were addressed to specific, already-existing Christian communities and the context makes clear that the authors of those epistles, including St. Paul, considered themselves as part of the larger Body of Christ. And a strong case has already been made by theologians that every doctrine of the Church is contained in Scripture, though sometimes in a way that is veiled or requiring the services of a logician, including the Immaculate Conception or dogma that Mary was untouched by original sin. The traditional interpretation of some translations of Luke 1:28 ("Hail, full of grace") is used as evidence for this teaching; another rather persuasive argument I once heard is that it would have been inappropriate or impossible for sin to give birth to sinlessness. But this belief was widely accepted as one of the "norms of the faithful" before its proclamation by papal authority in the last century; these facts have relevance to the question of celibacy.

Also seen by CORPUS as desperately needed is a reduction of the wide time gap between knowledge gained by psychology and sociology and its acceptance by the magisterium of the Church, a point made earlier in this book and also by Terry Dosh, co-founder of CORPUS, in a recent speech in the Baltimore area. During the course of writing his book, John Cornwell became familiar with the structure and character of the Vatican State. He describes it as an insular little enclave that is to a certain extent protected by its bureaucracy from much unwanted input from the outside world. Though it is necessary to heed the New Testament admonition to "prove all things; hold fast that which is good," more *aggiornamento* or openness still seems to be needed. Another reason the hierarchy have largely avoided this process of knowledge synthesis is a fear that they might be opening Pandora's box. But, as St. Thomas Aquinas understood with such clarity, the conflict between reason (science in modern terminology) and revelation is more apparent than real. What both Scripture and science tell us about the relationship between marriage and longevity is a case in point. There is a scientific basis for many Old Testament purity laws; for example, there is evidence that sexual intercourse during a woman's menstrual period sometimes causes endometriosis, a prime cause of infertility.

And physicians recommend at least a six-week period of sexual abstinence following childbirth. A strong case could also be made and probably supported by sociological and psychological studies both now and in the future (though study design might be difficult), that observance of traditional and Scripturally based Christian sexual morality promotes the health of both the individual and the society of which (s)he is a part. Deviation from Judeo-Christian sexual standards promotes individual unhappiness and loss of potential (for example, how much work stress and lessened productivity can be traced to the emotional fallout from divorce?) and eventually societal decay and dissolution. This is a reality that Evangelical thinkers such as Dr. James Dobson have long known and taught forcefully. We need not jettison the papacy or alter the Nicene Creed to learn much from other denominations; the greater outward enthusiasm and spirit of community found in much Evangelical worship has already been mentioned.

There is a continuing awareness among the present leadership of CORPUS of the positive role of the papacy; like the monarchy in some countries, the existence of this central figure has served to promote unity and doctrinal stability. But, as King Louis XIV of France reportedly said, "Apres moi, le deluge." Many of the younger resigned priests are less conservative and if reform is too long delayed, their energies could be turned in a more radical direction.

The lack of respect, even exploitation, that women have traditionally experienced in Catholic churches has contributed to the growth of radical feminism within that denomination. If change is too late in coming the result could be the total fragmentation of the American church, with eventual international consequences. If change occurs sooner, these groups will become marginalized with limited influence, or may even be drawn back into the mainstream.

Of course, the continuance of this rule is also an additional and unnecessary obstacle to ecumenism or the unity between Christian denominations. Change in this rule would be regarded as a significant concession and would help to reduce the mistrust that has accumulated because of the perception that the Roman Catholic Church is susceptible to the temptation to abuse its power. Evidence of flexibility on nonessential matters often leads to more substantive agreement, or at least an enhanced ability to cooperate in confronting the problems of the day. Christians are slowly coming to realize that their real opponents are competing or antagonistic philosophies such as secular humanism, not other Christians or even always those of other religious persuasions.

In the Catholic Church as it now exists, the pope usually provides not only leadership but the agenda as well. During John Paul's pontificate so far the bishops as a whole have failed to approach the question of celibacy with objectivity, or to deal with it at all. One retired bishop told me in a letter that the "high level authority of the Church is more inclined to hide from the problems raised (by celibacy) than to face up to them, even if they do seem insoluble." Though Cardinal O'Connor of New York did meet with a group of resigned priests after an ordination of some already-married clergy converts in January, 1990, his secretary wrote me in August of the same year that "His Eminence has consistently reiterated the teaching of the Holy Father upholding mandatory celibacy for priests of the Roman rite." However, at the time of the meeting with the resigned priests the Cardinal made the following observations: "It would be foolish to see this as a discipline that could never change. . . . It would be uncharitable, unjust and very naive and foolish to say that the sense of hurt on the part of Roman Catholic priests who married and cannot come back is groundless."[107]

The reiteration of the word "discipline" in connection with celibacy raises an obvious point: marriage requires discipline too.

Despite the Pope's directive, in June of 1990 a group of five bishops, who were having a national meeting at the University of Santa Clara, did meet with some resigned priest members of CORPUS. The dialogue was reported on the floor of the CORPUS convention scheduled at nearby San Jose State University and the attitude toward the meeting was generally positive. However, another papal directive has since been issued and communication has again been broken off.

The proceedings of the World Synod of Bishops held in the Vatican in October, 1990 have also not been encouraging. Though some individual bishops expressed a wish for change, mandatory celibacy was included in a

---

[107] CORPUS Reports, March-April 1990.

document on priestly formation and approved by a two-thirds majority. It may be significant however that the rule was not voted on separately, as has been done in previous years.[108] But rather than impartiality or even openness, the attitude seems to have been one of a frantic grasping for data to support a position already taken. There has been almost a juggling of statistics in the Synod's report that "the number of students for the priesthood has risen 53 percent in the last thirteen years." Less emphasized was the fact that this increase only applies to certain countries: the mission areas of India and Africa, where celibacy is in a sense a counter-cultural novelty and the negative effects haven't yet been seen, and possibly Brazil, Argentina and the Philippines.[109] However, a total of 16,500 priests resigned in the last decade and 312 left in 1989. The most that can be said is that the rate of decrease has slowed, though this is not yet certain. And with the possible exceptions of India (where there still aren't that many Catholics) and Africa, no place does the gain in vocations keep pace with the population growth, or with the number of priests who retire or die. The bishops seem to be counting on a program of improved spiritual formation for seminarians; the most that seems realistic to expect from such a program is a greater degree of commitment among new priests and possibly fewer departures after ordination, not necessarily more candidates. But the bishops seem to

[108] *Catholic Review.*
[109] *Catholic Review.*

be refusing or discounting such common sense input; "that's the way we've always done things."

Archbishop Pio Laghi expressed an opinion, apparently also held by the Pope, that the vocation crisis in Western Europe and the United States is caused mainly by materialism. Apparently overlooked was the fact that surveys have shown that 68 percent of Catholics in the United States and 53 percent of Italian Catholics favor optional celibacy. But why this tendency to discount public opinion in the United States? Public virtue is far from dead in our country, as witness the determination and resilience of the pro-life movement nationwide. Members of Operation Rescue continue to risk physical injury and financial loss on behalf of unborn children and the statewide referendum on the state's liberal abortion law scheduled for the fall of 1992 demonstrates that there is still hope for the people of Maryland. American Catholics still have a tradition of devotion and a high percentage of regular church attendance; they also have an average educational level that is above the national norm. This makes them less inclined to give equal weight to every papal teaching or directive. Not everything is *ex cathedra* or infallible; this concept is theologically sound and should not be written off as liberalism, and the historical context of rules cannot be disregarded. For example, some popes in the Middle Ages applied the Old Testament literally to current economic conditions and lending money at interest was prohibited as usury. However, this was later abandoned because it interfered with economic development. Another pope condemned the astronomy of Galileo; a few years ago, the Vatican issued an apology. However, with most American Catholics the awareness of these facts is simply realism, not rejection of the papacy; the Scripture text in which Christ says to Peter (then Simon): "You are Peter (Rock) and on this rock I will build my Church"[110] is still regularly read from our pulpits. There is a small number of extreme liberals, mainly in academic circles, who seem intent on rejecting Scripture and Church tradition in favor of their own theories, but they do not reflect the views of the great majority of ordinary Catholics in places like Boston, Baltimore and Columbus, Ohio. But creeping (and sometimes galloping) secularism is the real enemy in our country, though materialism is a problem as well, and mandatory celibacy is no longer an effective form of Christian witness—if indeed it ever was.

When Americans see a need for change, they should be taken seriously, not written off as merely materialistic. This is a sophisticated form of the *argumentum ad hominem:* attacking your opponent personally as a means of discrediting his message. Though the Church can never be a democracy in matters of doctrine, public opinion polls on issues such as celibacy should be viewed with respect as a possible indicator of the way the Holy Spirit may be leading. A possible temporary solution might be for bishops to be permitted to ordain married men in countries that are both experiencing clergy shortage and where the will of the people favors change or at least seems receptive. This would not be a perma-

---

[110] Matthew 16:18.

nent solution but might prepare the way for worldwide change.

As the letter from the retired bishop suggests, a larger barrier to change than theology may be an unwillingness to confront the structural, practical and even economic restructuring that a married priesthood would entail. The Synod would have been a valuable opportunity to start to examine these issues and perhaps to begin the dialogue with other Churches suggested by John Paul I. The practical obstacles to change may in fact be overestimated. In an effort to provide a beginning on these matters, I decided to interview some married clergymen of other denominations, also a married priest, Father Steve Sutton, who left the Anglican Church approximately eight years ago. Other useful information emerged, but there were two major focuses of my questions: the role of the pastor's wife and the pastor's use of time and how he manages to combine family and ministry. As reiterated by Cardinal O'Connor, one obstacle to change is the perception that a priest is too busy for family life. If that is indeed true, a chief contributing factor is again the shortage of priests.

All four clergymen were helpful and cooperative. I first spoke with Pastor Leo Richter at Christ the King Lutheran Church in Baltimore County. Rev. Richter mentioned an emerging emphasis in his denomination in recent years on time management. Family and ministry are seen as equal in importance, though in earlier years the focus has been on ministry as a priority. One suggested solution to the problem of how to find time for everything which he himself follows is to divide his day into three segments of four hours each. He devotes one segment each day to his wife and children and also tries to take one day off each week. Rev. Richter admits that time management is sometimes not an easy task, but he feels it is worth the effort. Having a family forces him to be organized in his use of time; the positive input his family offers also helps him to avoid burnout.

The next married clergyman I interviewed was Father Robert Stucky at St. Mark's-On-The-Hill Episcopal Church, also in Baltimore County. He volunteered the perception that he is "a better and more sensitive priest by virtue of his marriage"; he has a wife and two children. Fr. Stucky also admitted a certain tension in juggling ministry and family, but thinks it is worth the effort; the aim is the achievement of balance. He tries to spend part of each day with his family; Mondays are his usual day off. He indicated the need for some privacy for the priest's family and that a clear role for the spouse needed to be delineated in any particular parish assignment. Priests' wives in his denomination vary in what ministries or duties they assume; there are a wide variety of possibilities including the Altar Guild, Sunday School and choir. Some wives may decide against involvement in any specific ministry other than hospitality; his wife helps to organize a monthly parish dinner. The Episcopal and Anglican denominations have been able to maintain a monastic tradition as well as a married priesthood; further information on the Anglican monastic tradition was also supplied by Fr. Steve Sutton. "A sort of natural selection takes place," Fr. Stucky said, regarding which candidates for ministry choose marriage and which choose the monastic tradition. The Anglican Church has both active and contemplative religious communities. The active orders are involved in a variety of ministries, including teaching and work with the hungry and homeless. Fr. Stucky stated that the contemplatives take permanent vows; the vows taken by those in active orders tend to be renewable. In regard to the difficulties the Catholic Church is currently having with celibacy, Fr. Stucky volunteered his opinion that change should be forthcoming: "How much worse does it have to get?"

I next spoke with Fr. Constantine Monios, the pastor of Baltimore's Greek Orthodox Cathedral of the Annunciation. He mentioned that in his denomination and especially in the United States, the married priest is preferred because it is felt that he "understands life better", especially family issues, and is thus "better able to serve his people." There are however a number of unmarried priests in Greece, also some in Jerusalem. The Greek Orthodox Church has been able to maintain a cloistered monastic tradition and also has a small number of hermits. The main role of a priest's wife in his denomination is seen as that of wife and mother; she does not always serve in specific ministries. Fr. Monios is a busy man; he is one of only two priests in his large congregation and gets only six vacation days a year. He tries to make time each morning for his wife and family. A priest in his denomination is expected to marry before ordination, as it is felt that a priest who is involved in dating might create certain difficulties for his congregation: for example, if an engagement were broken. This raises the issue of a possibly difficult transition stage for those already ordained if the rule were changed; as a single person with some experience, I am of the opinion that it is possible for a clergyman to engage in dating if he does so discreetly and is careful to observe Christian sexual morality, with a goal of marriage and getting to know a specific individual, not sexual activity.

I last spoke with Father Steve Sutton who had left the Episcopal Church to become a Catholic priest seven years previously. His ordination was accepted and it was mainly a matter of taking a few courses at Catholic University. Fr. Steve has been married more than 22 years and has three children; the oldest is age 15. The Church of which he is the associate pastor, St. Joseph's in the Fullerton area of Baltimore County, is the fastest-growing in the area and now has more than 3,900 families. He has been well-accepted by parishioners and fellow priests alike and "no one has told (him) anything negative to (his) face". In addition to being a parish priest, he teaches a Bible class at a local Catholic high school. His wife, Barbara, also works full time; they do not live in the rectory. His wife is a Eucharistic minister. Fr. Sutton sees the first qualification of a pastor's wife as that of being "a committed Christian" and "supportive of her husband in the demands on his time." Each priest in the parish has a weekly day off; they divide the week between them, with some latitude for emergencies. Fr. Sutton mentioned that accompanying the mostly married priesthood is a monastic tradition in the Anglican Church; there are a total of 33 religious orders in the United States. There are also a small number of Anglican or Episcopal priests who feel personally called to celibacy and take a separate vow unconnected to the ordination process.

Fr. Sutton feels he is a better priest because of his family, as there is a psychological need for intimacy and his family are effective "counterbalances" to his work. Fr. Sutton states frankly (his Anglican heritage gives him some perspective too) that change in the rule of celibacy is "an idea whose time has come."

Fr. Sutton was the priest at the Sunday Mass I later attended; it was a memorable experience. The large semicircular sanctuary was filled, including the balcony, and there were a number of young families with children. The people sang and participated with real joy and there was obvious warmth at the greeting of peace. There was a definite sense of being part of the people of God and also of a worshipping community. The church has an active social action program, including aid to the homeless and a pro-life committee. There is also an adult education committee, a Charismatic prayer group and a prayer "hot line" for people with special needs. The November, 1990 election was coming up in two days; without breaking any rules regarding the endorsement of specific candidates, Fr. Sutton did encourage the people to vote.

Like Fr. Sutton, my background as a convert to the Catholic Church gives me a different perspective on celibacy. I made the decision in my teen years; I had been attending the Disciples of Christ Church (former President Reagan's denomination) in the small town of Turlock, California. Though I found I could not accept the

theology of this church, one of my most positive memories
concerns the married pastor, Primus Bennett, and his
wife. As human beings, they were not immune to the
occasional spat or disagreement, but were always united
in the service of the Church. Mrs. Bennett was the choir
director and made several home visits to our family. My
mother, who joined the Catholic Church several years
ago, was raised in this denomination.

From this brief examination of the experience of
married clergymen, it should be clear that the dichotomy
the church has created between priesthood and family
life—that the priest simply doesn't have time for both—is
an artificial one. All four of the clergymen I interviewed
reported that marriage and family have enhanced their
ministry; some denominations either prefer or require a
married clergyman. The Greek Orthodox position has
already been mentioned; the Wesleyan Methodists do not
permit the ordination of single men.

It seems likely too that these denominations have
established methods for dealing with clergy who deviate
from Christian sexual morality. The potential for positive
Christian witness of a happily married clergyman has
already been mentioned; there is, of course, negative
potential as well in the case of a clergyman who divorces,
is involved in an irregular marriage or who engages in
illicit sexual activity. However, with more available
clergy, the Church would be in a stronger position to
require that they maintain exemplary standards.

Some specific regulations will no doubt evolve, but it
seems reasonable to expect that a married priest must be
in a canonically valid marriage and that it should be to

another Catholic. Though some lay people manage to bring it off, a "mixed marriage" would seemingly present too many difficulties for a priest. In keeping with the sacramental and permanent character of marriage as established by Christ, except in unusual circumstances (there are some canonically valid grounds for annulment, in other words, a sacramental Christian marriage did not exist) divorce and remarriage would disqualify a priest from ministry. The Greek Orthodox require that their priests be married only once, also preventing widowers who remarry from returning to the ministry, though this may be a little extreme. I suspect that an analysis of the historical context of the New Testament admonition that bishops must be "married but once" would reveal that this was actually a prohibition of polygamy, not remarriage after the death of a spouse. This view would seem to contradict the totality of Jesus' teaching, which emphasizes both the indissolubility of marriage and the ending of that commitment by death. Historically, many Christian widowed persons have seen that state as an opportunity for a more exclusive service of God, but to make this an institutional requirement might lead us back into the same sort of trap from which we are attempting to escape. Promotions in the Church hierarchy (from priest to bishop for example) should be given on the basis of merit, moral integrity and ability, not marital status. But clearly delineated expectations would serve as a motivation to priests to maintain positive family lives and perhaps to seek timely professional intervention in the event of serious problems.

From my years of experience as a marriage counselor, I can report that most divorces are not inevitable, though there is a certain percentage of marriages that probably should not have taken place. Marriage breakdown in general reflects a lack of effort or commitment by one or both parties. It has significance too that the spouses of doctors have been notorious for their complaints regarding the overcommitment of physicians to their work and corresponding lack of time for family; however, physicians also have one of the lowest divorce rates of any occupational group. Divorce is avoided because of its potential to disrupt the physician's work and status in the community. Also, the trend toward group practice, in which all members of a group of physicians are familiar with the patients and have a rotating schedule of being on duty, is a help to doctors in their efforts to balance their professional and family commitments. With the acceptance of marrieds for ordination and the acceptance back into ministry of resigned priests who wish to return, it would seem possible to assign several priests to every parish and still select the best-qualified candidates. Combinations of full and part-time clergy might be workable, with corresponding salary adjustments. And the Church would stop having to take up so many collections for the support of retirees! Most married women work during part or all of their married years; this trend seems irreversible.

Though there might be a transitional period involving considerable confusion, it should still be remembered that celibacy is a vocation from God for some people and this also has value. As in the Anglican tradition, a priest who feels called to this (or rather the Evangelical Counsels as a total life-style, not celibacy specifically) should make separate vows not connected to his ordination. Such a person should be expected to join a religious community if possible or an effort should be made to place him in assignment in an area where he does have some family ties to offer emotional support. There is no reason to fear that a predominately married clergy would signal the death of the Church's monastic tradition; this has not been the case in other churches. Some communities would probably go out of existence, but this is already happening. Others would probably be strengthened by possibly smaller numbers of applicants who at the same time have a greater degree of commitment. The contemplative tradition would certainly continue, but some of the active orders might want to experiment with renewable vows. This policy might have several positive results, including more applicants with a higher degree of enthusiasm. The Daughters of Charity of St. Vincent de Paul is the largest women's order in the Church; they have been very successful with this model.

But the Holy Spirit leads in different ways at different times; the effects of the monastic tradition in the Church have been mixed. It has undoubtedly helped to make the Catholic Church strong in an institutional sense, but has also had the effect of reducing the involvement of the laity and perhaps of preventing many from developing their full faith potential. Until the post-Vatican II years, many lay people felt like "second class Catholics"; this is something I have heard from several sources.

To recall the words of Fr. Stucky, when celibacy is not mandated, a process of natural selection takes place in which the person is able to discern and act upon the Will of God in his or her individual life. This process of discernment is the basic issue for Christians, the key to personal holiness, and also the best guarantee that they will spend their lives effectively. Marital status *per se* is a secondary issue and is in fact an artificial distinction imposed by the Church's current rules. As St. Paul says, "I should like you to be as I am. Still, each one has his own gift from God, one this and another that."[111]

It is my opinion that a priest should be strongly encouraged and probably required, to choose either marriage or an avowed celibate life within a reasonable period of time, for example, within five years after ordination. Such a rule would still allow the seminary to be primarily a place of prayer and spiritual formation, though a total prohibition of dating might be unwise. Membership in a secular institute, a form of religious life that has been developed in this century, is another alternative for priests who feel personally called to celibacy. Members of secular institutes make the three vows of poverty, chastity and obedience (frequently with some modification of poverty and obedience to suit preexisting life commitments) but do not live in community. Many secular institutes, the Voluntas Dei Institute for example, do schedule regular meetings for the sharing of prayer and life experience, but the wide dispersal of

---

[111] 1 Corinthians 7:7.

members makes it difficult to do so frequently. Membership in a secular institute should not in most cases be seen as obviating more immediate sources of emotional support such as the priest's extended family. Those candidates for ordination who feel personally called to the Evangelical Counsels (and those who plan to undertake a life of prayer or work in foreign missions might be encouraged in that direction) could still choose to begin their priesthood formation as members of religious communities, or that option would be available to them after ordination.

But an indefinite continuation of single life, with the stresses of dating and increased vulnerability to life's problems, is not really compatible with the peace of mind and religious commitment a priest must have to serve effectively. A rule requiring a life-style decision within a certain period of time might be a greater safeguard against sexual scandals, including those caused by non-abstinent homosexuals, than psychological testing alone, but in this imperfect world no single safeguard or combination of them is likely to be 100 percent effective. But the basic point is that we as Catholics can learn much from the practice of other denominations and still develop an approach to change that is compatible with our needs and traditions.

Richard Sipe quotes theologian Fr. Patrick Granfield's paraphrasing of official Church teaching: "The Christian faithful have the right and 'even at times a duty' to make known their opinions to bishops and to other Christian faithful on matters which pertain to the good of the Church." This sense of the faithful is also one of the norms of theological truth.[112] The Holy Spirit also resides in the hierarchy of course, but when there is a vested interest in the *status quo,* it is more difficult to hear the "still small Voice."[113] If the "heavy winds" of controversy and division are permitted to begin, it may not be possible to hear the Voice at all.

It would not actually be a great exaggeration or oversimplification to reduce much of what has been said in this book to the following simple observed truth: the Catholic Church has a continuing choice to make: whether to preserve the rule of celibacy or to preserve the Church. It cannot preserve both indefinitely and so far has been making the wrong choice.

The vested interest of the hierarchy in resisting change has two main components: a reluctance to confront the structural changes that would be required and a reluctance to confront the issue on a personal level; though a not completely foreseeable degree of institutional restructuring must take place, this issue is ultimately and unavoidably an intensely personal one as well.

Though there will always be a place for the Scripturally based monastic tradition, the "celibate countercultural witness" of mandatory celibacy extolled by the Synod of Bishops in fact no longer exists. In contrast, there seems to be a movement of the Holy Spirit among laypeople that favors change and that transcends group affiliation, or conservatism vs. liberalism. Such disparate

---

[112] Sipe, p. 288.
[113] 1 Kings 19:12.

elements as academia and the Charismatic Renewal would like to see optional celibacy or at least have an open mind about it. The heart of the dilemma—that the hierarchy currently appears to be saying that maintenance of this rule is more important than the people's right to the Eucharist—is being perceived by an increasing number of lay people and will escalate to the level of scandal and mass defection if change is not forthcoming. Some interpretations of membership statistics of the Catholic Church in the United States would suggest that the decline has already begun. If the governing structure of the Church continue to ignore the will of the people, the inevitable result will be a growing attitude of anticlericalism among the laity, and increasing isolation and estrangement of clergy at all levels from the people they serve. This has already occurred in other western countries, most notably France and Mexico; the effect of anticlericalism on the Church's Christian witness and ability to influence society in these countries has been lethal.

During the recent Synod, Cardinal Lucas Moreira Neves from Brazil (one of the few countries experiencing a vocation increase) spelled out the problem—increasing divergence between hierarchy and people—in unmistakable terms: "Celibacy cannot be separated from priestly life—even though the worldwide priest shortage can lead to the 'temptation' of suggesting the ordination of married men."[114] This intransigence over a mere rule

---

[114] *Catholic Review,* October 17, 1990.

and one without even a clear Scriptural mandate, recalls what has been said earlier; the real "temptation" may not be compromise of standards or the Gospel message, but women and sexuality!

An increasing number of Catholic publications are beginning to spot the inconsistency or out-of-order priorities. The following is a quote from the June, 1990 issue of Eucharistic Minister:

> Finally, the third question raised in this situation asks how much of a 'right' the parish has to the full and authentic celebration of the Eucharist. If this liturgy is both the source and summit of the Church's life, then we are substituting a pale imitation. Could this arrangement be the liturgical equivalent of junk food? Because only male celibates are called to priestly orders in the Roman rite of the Church this third question leads, naturally, to a consideration of how much weight maleness and celibacy carry in relation to the Eucharist. At what point does the balance tip? . . . We are stepping off into territory that is strange to us. There are no maps except the old ones. There is no guide except the Spirit. There is no consolation in refusing to face the future because in the land that lies before us are buried . . . immense treasures. We will not find them by standing still.

The task, which seemingly can only be performed by the laity and later ratified by the Church's governing structure, is twofold: to produce a change in policy allowing a married priesthood and to do so in a timely manner before disaster strikes; this seems preventable if action is begun now. The damage to the Church if change does not occur is inevitable and will take two forms: priestless parishes with corresponding changes in the Church's form of worship (historically speaking, such changes have also tended to be irreversible) and destruction of the Church's credibility in a world that is increasingly rejecting of Christianity.

The laity must make their voices heard as loudly and frequently as possible if these results are to be prevented; the goal of influencing the next Synod of Bishops in the year 2000 should be kept in mind. Methods for making themselves heard include discussion of this book by parish groups, letters to both Catholic and secular publications, and letters to local bishops. Parents whose sons may be considering the priesthood but who are reluctant to surrender them to the hazards and stresses of forced celibacy are in a position to write very effectively to local seminaries and bishops. (The priesthood—as currently designed by the church—can be hazardous to your health.) Even radio talk shows can be usefully employed by a caller who is courteous and reasonably well-informed, and this is the sort of topic that tends to generate interest. The public opinion polls have provided a beginning but widespread *personal* involvement by individuals and by parish groups remains an absolute necessity.

If the American and Canadian bishops *as a bloc* were to advocate change, and they would probably be joined by others, this might serve to open channels of communication with the Vatican. This is similar to what occurred in the last century when the doctrine of the Immaculate

Conception was made an article of faith. But as was alluded to earlier, this *ex cathedra* proclamation was made in response to a movement of the Holy Spirit among the rank-and-file and was an official endorsement, as it were, of long-established belief. It is obviously less difficult to proclaim the doctrine of the Immaculate Conception than to change the rule of celibacy, but the faithful seem to have a certain sense that the difficulties are being exaggerated. Archbishop Weakland of Milwaukee has already published a pastoral letter suggesting the ordination of selected married men as probably the only solution to the clergy shortage and has asked for feedback from the people of his archdiocese.

As the lessons of history make clear, Christ's promise of generalized immunity to his Church from "the gates of hell" does not extend to every country; human error and stubbornness still play a part. Hopefully, T.S. Elliot wasn't referring to the Western Catholic Church in his poem "The Hollow Men": "This is the way the world ends, this is the way the world ends, this is the way the world ends; not with a bang but with a whimper."

Anthony Padovano, the previous president of CORPUS, has likened the rule of mandatory celibacy in the Church to the Berlin Wall. It was dismantled very quickly and piece by piece, but a great number of people were involved.

THE PEOPLE WANT CHANGE and they must make it happen.

Questions for discussion or consideration:

1) Jesus warns us against the potentially deadly spiritual effects of excessive human attachments: "If your right eye . . . right hand is your trouble, cut it off and throw it away! Better to lose part of your body than to have it all cast into Gehenna."[115] Because of its long history in the Catholic Church and their personal commitment to it, are the hierarchy too attached to the rule of celibacy? Does this rule have the potential to destroy the whole Body of Christ?[116]

2) What does Jesus' parable about "the tree and its fruit"[117] say about mandatory celibacy and its effects in today's Church?

---

[115] Matthew 5:29-30.
[116] In bringing about change of this magnitude, prayer is indispensable. The writer fasts and prays (the church fast and the sorrowful mysteries of the Rosary) the first Friday of each month.
[117] Matthew 7:18-20.

Bibliography

1) Archdiocese of Baltimore, *The Catholic Review,* Oct. 17, 1990; Oct. 24, 1990; Oct. 31, 1990.

2) Coleman, James, *Abnormal Psychology and Modern Life,* Glenview, Illinois: Scott, Foresman and Company, third edition, 1964.

3) Cornwell, John A., *A Thief in the Night: the Mysterious Death of Pope John Paul I,* New York: Simon and Schuster, 1989.

4) CORPUS (Corps of Reserve Priests Organized for Service) Research Document I: Minneapolis, Minnesota: CORPUS, 1988.

5) CORPUS Reports, vol. 16, no. 2, March-April, 1990; September-October, 1990.

6) *Encyclopedia Americana,* Danbury, Connecticut, Grolier Inc., 1990, vol. 15.

7) *Encyclopedia Britannica,* Inc., Chicago: London: Toronto: William Benton, publisher, 1959, vols. 1, 10, 13, 14, 21.

8) *Eucharistic Minister,* June, 1990.

9) Eugene Kennedy and Victor Heckler, *The Loyola Psychological Study of the Ministry and Life of the American Priest,* April 1971, National Conference of Catholic Bishops.

10) Lidz, Theodore, *The Person: His Development Throughout the Life Cycle,* New York: Basic Books, Inc., 1977.

11) Lynch, James J., *The Broken Heart: the Medical Consequences of Loneliness,* New York: Basic Books, Inc., 1977.

12) Lynch, James J., *The Language of the Heart: the Body's Response to Human Dialogue,* New York: Basic Books, Inc., 1985.

13) *National Enquirer,* 1990.

14) Ranke-Heinemann, Uta, *Eunuchs for the Kingdom of Heaven,* New York: Doubleday, 1990.

15) Ripley's "Believe It Or Not" Museum, San Antonio, Texas.
16) Sipe, Richard, *A Secret World: Sexuality and the Search for Celibacy*, New York: Brunner/Mazel, Inc., 1990.
17) Sanford, John, *Ministry Burnout*, Mahwah, New Jersey: Paulist Press, 1982.
18) The Bishops' Committee on Priestly Life and Ministry, "The Priest and Stress," Washington, D.C.: United States Catholic Conference, 1982.
19) *The Catholic Encyclopedia*, Nashville, Tennessee: Thomas Nelson Publishers, 1987.
20) *The New American Bible*, Chicago, Illinois: J.G. Ferguson Publishing Co., 1971.
21) *The New American Bible for Catholics*, Iowa Falls, Iowa: World Bible Publishers, 1970: New Testament revised 1986.
22) *Time* magazine: various issues, 1990; August 19, 1991.
23) "Women," *Time* magazine, special fall issue, 1990.

Additional copies of this book may be obtained
from your local bookstore,
or by sending $11.95 per paperback copy, postpaid,
$16.95 per library hardcover copy, postpaid,
to:

New Paradigm Books
P.O. Box 60008
Pasadena, CA 91116

CA residents kindly add 8% sales tax

FAX orders to: (818) 792-2121

Telephone VISA/MC orders to: (800) 326-2671